THE ORIENT OBSERVED

IMAGES OF THE MIDDLE EAST
FROM THE SEARIGHT COLLECTION

THE ORIENT OBSERVED

IMAGES OF THE MIDDLE EAST
FROM THE SEARIGHT COLLECTION

by
Briony Llewellyn

The Victoria & Albert Museum

Cover Illustrations
Front: Amadeo Preziosi, *The Entrance to the Golden Horn, Constantinople* (detail).
Back: Carl Haag, *War*.

British Library Cataloguing-in-Publication Data available

Published by the Victoria and Albert Museum 1989 in association with
Shell International Petroleum Company Ltd
Copyright of Text © Briony Llewellyn
Copyright of Images © The Trustees of the Victoria and Albert Museum

ISBN 1 85177 003 8

Designed by Brian Denyer

Printed by the Roundwood Press Ltd

The Victoria and Albert Museum gratefully acknowledges the support
given by Shell International Petroleum Company Ltd, not only in helping
to make possible the acquisition of the Searight Collection, but also in
producing this publication on its behalf to accompany the 1989 exhibition.

Contents

For Roddy and Theresa

Foreword

I am glad that the Searight Collection will receive wider attention and appreciation with the publication of this book. In it many of the finest works in the Collection are illustrated and described in the hope that the reader will glimpse something of the wealth and variety of the Collection's numerous watercolours, drawings, prints and books of interest to researchers and connoisseurs alike.

Since 1931 when Rodney Searight first went to Egypt, the countries portrayed in his Collection have undergone an incredible transformation. This has in many ways benefited their peoples but, inevitably with such fundamental changes and developments, there has been upheaval and disruption to the traditional way of life. Those who mourn the loss of cultural identity and heritage in a region that more than any other has a deep sense of history will find some consolation in the Searight Collection (now preserved intact for posterity in the Victoria and Albert Museum), since it helps to document aspects of this heritage that might otherwise have been forgotten.

Not only did Rodney Searight have a distinguished career with Shell, but he is also an inspired connoisseur and a gifted amateur artist who has turned his moments of relaxation to an excellent and original purpose.

I commend this book to all who have an interest in the people, architecture, topography, art and history of the Middle East.

Sir Peter Holmes
Chairman
The "Shell" Transport and Trading Company, p.l.c.

Editorial Note

The text accompanying the illustrations is based on the catalogue of the Searight Collection published on COMfiche in conjunction with the colour and black and white microfiche illustrations of the entire collection. The Searight Collection forms Part I-III of *The Muslim World*, a microfiche, produced by Emmett Publishing Limited, of images of the Middle East by European artists, housed in the Department of Designs, Prints and Drawings at the Victoria and Albert Museum.

The transliteration of Arabic, Persian and Turkish place and personal names always presents a thorny problem, especially when dealing with writers and artists of the eighteenth and nineteenth centuries who transcribed names phonetically and therefore variably. To use their spelling in the text would have caused confusion. In general therefore the widely accepted old British Museum system for Arabic transliteration has been adopted, but without accents. Turkish names and words are spelt in the way nowadays established in Turkey, except where a Europeanised form has become established, such as *odalisque* for *odalic*.

An important deviation from modern forms and spelling is in several well-known place names. Since this book deals almost exclusively with pre-First World War artists and travellers, the terms that they would have used and known have been adopted: Persia for Iran; Mesopotamia for Iraq; Palestine or the Holy Land for the area divided between Israel and that which it now occupies; Constantinople for Istanbul; Smyrna for Izmir; Thebes for the west bank at Luxor, and so on.

For the same reason, Near East, in preference to Middle East, a term coined only in the early twentieth century, has been used in the text accompanying the illustrations. The nowadays more familiar Middle East has been used in the Title, Foreword, Preface and Introduction. Orient or oriental is used throughout to describe the area between North Africa and India, and does not include what we now describe as the Far East.

Abbreviations after an artist's name are as follows:

FLS	Fellow of the the Linnaean Society
FRGS	Fellow of the Royal Geographical Society
FRIBA	Fellow of the Royal Institute of British Architects
FRS	Fellow of the Royal Society
FSA	Fellow of the Society of Antiquaries
NWS	New Water Colour Society
OWS	Old Water Colour Society
P	President
RA	Royal Academy
RBA	Society of British Artists
RI	Royal Institute of Painters in Water Colours
RWS	Royal Society of Painters in Water Colours

As far as possible the artists' titles are used except where the spelling or phrasing would cause confusion; in these cases modern transliteration has been substituted.

The works are on white, cream or beige wove paper, unless otherwise stated; the medium is specified in each case. Dimensions refer to the area covered by the image, drawn or printed, on the sheet (unless otherwise specified), and are given in centimetres, height before width. Inscriptions are transcribed literally and given in italics.

Further information about the work, such as provenance, exhibitions and literature, are to be found in the COMfiche catalogue of the Searight Collection, available in the Print Room, Department of Designs, Prints and Drawings, at the Victoria and Albert Museum.

Preface

Ten years ago I went to Rodney Searight's flat in London seeking information and illustrations for an article on artists who had visited Petra in the nineteenth century. Mine was one of many requests he received for assistance on a particular topic relating to western artists in the Middle East, and with me, as with others, he was both patient and constructive. He had laid out a huge book of lithographs by Léon de Laborde, two splendid watercolours by Edward Lear and W.H. Bartlett (both illustrated in this book, pp. 46 and 47), and a couple of his 'curiosities': a view of the theatre at Petra apparently derived from Laborde via Roberts, and another of the Khasnah, by an unidentified artist. We discussed these and other images at length and I went away bemused, dimly aware that here was a rich and vast mine of information on numerous aspects of European involvement in the Middle East.

I wrote my article (for *The Connoisseur),* adding views of Sinai to those of Petra. But that was by no means the end of my connection with the Searight Collection. During several more visits Roddy gave me a brief run through his extraordinary collection of watercolours, drawings, prints and books, which seemed to fill almost every inch of wall space, every drawer and every cupboard in his large flat. Bitten by the same bug that had evidently bitten him, I began to delve into the highways and byways of the collection. Several exhibitions and publications resulted from our collaboration during the early 1980s, dealing with a variety of artists, among them William Müller, Luigi Mayer, and Frank Dillon, and themes (see p.145). Always Roddy was unfailingly generous, not only lending many much-loved treasures to these exhibitions, sometimes for several months at a time, but also sharing his vast fund of knowledge about the works and their artists. For, with almost every acquisition of a drawing, print or book, he had researched its artist, and its subject, with the result that each one was documented, sometimes with notes extending to several pages. Without this information as a base to work from, the task of compiling a formal catalogue when, in 1985, the collection was acquired by the Victoria and Albert Museum, would have been much more difficult and time-consuming.

The Searight Collection is unique as a pictorial record of the cultural interaction between the West and the Middle East before the widespread use of photography. Portraying a range of scenes, events and personalities of the Islamic world through the eyes of over 700 artists, writers and travellers, it is unrivalled in its extent and variety. It is perhaps also unique in its inception and development. In the 1960s when it was begun, interest in the subject was confined to a mere handful of academics and collectors, but during the 1970s, the period of the collection's fastest growth, 'Orientalism' suddenly became fashionable. This was due mainly to the oil boom, which meant that not only the Arab nations but also the Europeans who went to work in the oil-rich countries became aware of and able to acquire western artists' portrayals of the Middle East. Rodney Searight's collection played a part in sustaining this demand at the same time as benefitting from it as more and more Orientalist paintings, drawings and prints came on to the fine art market. By the end of the 1970s sky-high prices slowed down the rate and volume of his acquisitions, although his knowledge and instinct still enabled him to make several more significant additions to his collection.

This book is intended as an introduction to Rodney Searight's great collection. It is not a survey of Orientalism in general, nor does it explore any particular aspect of it in depth, but in grouping the images by subject rather than by date or place it focusses on a few of the themes running through the collection and thus indicates some of the issues that preoccupied western artists and travellers in the Middle East.

Throughout this book I have relied heavily on Rodney Searight's notes in the Searight Archive in the Victoria and Albert Museum, and on the research and cataloguing of the collection undertaken at the Museum by Tanya Szrajber, Jenny Elkan and myself, and now published on COMfiche as part of *The Muslim World* (Emmett Publishing Ltd.). During the compilation of this catalogue we sought advice from many specialists in a variety of fields; they are too numerous to list here but they are acknowledged with thanks in the COMfiche catalogue.

I am indebted to several other people who have assisted me with this book. Above all, Charles Newton, Curator in the Department of Designs, Prints and Drawings at the V&A, himself an expert in the field of Orientalism, especially in relation to Turkey, has provided advice and support far beyond the call of duty. As well as being closely involved with the cataloguing of the collection for the COMfiche, he assisted in the selection for this book, commented on my text, and gave immeasurable other practical help. Sarah Searight, a Middle East specialist and author of *The British in the Middle East,* has, throughout this project, been ready with her support, and has also given invaluable academic and practical assistance. Two people in particular have contributed their expertise to several of my descriptions of the illustrations: Peter Stocks of the British Library, Oriental Collections, and co-author of the Blue Guide on Egypt; and Jennifer M. Scarce, Curator of Eastern Costumes, National Museum of Scotland, Edinburgh, and author of *Women's Costume of the Near and Middle East.* For this publication, Krystyna Matyjaskiewicz kindly agreed, despite all her other committtments, to exercise her considerable editing skills on my text. Without the support of Shell International Petroleum Company Ltd., this publication would not have been possible. I am grateful to the individuals within the Company who have worked hard and patiently to produce it.

To all these people who have most generously given me their time and advice, I am enormously grateful. Any errors of fact, transliteration or syntax, however, are entirely mine. Finally I would like to thank my husband, and other members of my family circle, including Lucille Gale, who have, by helping me look after my two children, given me the time to write this book. BL

William Hogarth (1697-1764)
A Procession through the Hippodrome   1723
Etching; trimmed to 25.5 x 34.6 cm.

10

Recollections of a Collector

'Does he bowl or bat?', asked the Shell general manager in Cairo on my arrival in Egypt in March 1931 on my first overseas contract with Shell. Two days later I found myself making my first appearance on the cricket field at Gazirah Sporting Club in Cairo. This may seem an inappropriate beginning to the story of my subsequent absorption in collecting Middle Eastern drawings and watercolours. It marked, however, my introduction to an area where I was to spend much of my working life, and at least partly explains my interest in those who had travelled there before me and left so vivid a record of their impressions.

As time passed and I moved around the world, often in the Middle East, dwindling opportunities for indulging in the time consuming demands of the cricket field gave way to other hobbies – sketching, bird-watching and photography. My interest in painting and drawing arose from an aptitude for sketching or caricaturing whoever or whatever caught my eye. Prior to my departure for Egypt I had attended life classes at the Chelsea Polytechnic. Its discipline was to stay with me ever after in the form of dozens of sketch-books, dinner menus and any other scraps of paper that came to hand, reflecting my interest in places and people.

Soon I developed the habit of buying watercolours of familiar scenes – Albert Goodwin and George Clausen being among my early favourites – and life drawings by the great Victorian draughtsmen that took me back to my early disciplinary evenings at the Chelsea Poly. The Middle East hardly featured, except David Roberts's lithographs at a few pounds a time. In about 1960 I acquired a fine Roberts watercolour of Cairo (see p.68) from the Fine Art Society for the exorbitant price of £52 10s, a purchase I regard as the foundation of my collection. A week or two later I acquired an exquisite drawing by the great J.F. Lewis for £38. The Middle East was then an 'unpopular' area, and such drawings and watercolours as did appear were disgracefully cheap.

Slowly the Middle East bug bit. My return to England, and eventual retirement from Shell in 1966, created more time and opportunity for collecting. Advice and encouragement were copiously forthcoming from such friends as Dudley Snelgrove in the British Museum, Mrs Joey Barnden who devoted days in helping me to put my acquisitions on to cards, and many in the fine art trade. In the late 1960s the existence of the collection began to be known to publishers and authors seeking illustrations for books about the Middle East. A break-through came with the publication, by Weidenfeld & Nicolson in 1969, of my daughter Sarah's book, *The British in the Middle East*, largely illustrated from my collection. This was mainly due to the enthusiasm of Jacquemine Charlotte Lodwidge, Weidenfeld's picture researcher. The book sparked a new interest in the collection resulting in an exhibition at Leighton House in January 1971.

I live close to Leighton House and knew its oriental contents well. I also knew its then Curator, Denis Hartley, and he was familiar

Sir Robert Ker Porter (1777-1842)
Buonaparte Ordering Five Hundred & Eighty of his wounded Soldiers to be poisoned at Jaffa. 1803
Pen and brown ink, brown and grey washes; 29.7 x 27.5 cm.

with my collection. Thence sprang the idea of an exhibition that might attract visitors to the hitherto sadly neglected charms of Leighton House itself. In the event all our hopes and expectations were wildly exceeded. The press was enthusiastic and well over two thousand visitors made their unaccustomed way to Leighton House, thus putting the collection on the map. In so doing the exhibition provided just the sort of encouragement I needed – to persist in what could only be regarded at that time as a forgotten field. It was forgotten not only in terms of subject but also, and perhaps more significantly, in regard to the artists.

Glancing through the modest catalogue that I produced for the Leighton House exhibition, I am astonished today at the wide assemblage of British and foreign artists, both amateur and professional, that I had already brought together. The attractions that had drawn them to the Middle East had also drawn me to them – the architectural, archaeological, topographical and human

11

subjects so amply and satisfyingly available in that part of the world. Not all of the artists were British; among the foreigners were Giovanni Battista Borra, Luigi Mayer, Baron Dominique Vivant Denon, Adrien Dauzats, Prosper Marilhat, Linant de Bellefonds, Alexandre Gabriel Decamps, Carl Werner, Michel-François Préaulx, Count Amadeo Preziosi and the various members of the Schranz family. The British included David Roberts, J.F. Lewis as well as his younger brother F.C. Lewis Jr, Francis Arundale, Hercules Brabazon Brabazon, Owen Jones, W.H. Bartlett, William Simpson, Sir A.H. Layard, William Müller, Thomas Allom, Sir David Wilkie, Harry Johnson, William Wyld, William Page, William Purser, Elijah Walton, Sir John Tenniel, Sir George Hayter, Frederick and Edward Goodall, Selina Bracebridge, Count Albert Gleichen, Captain Robert Moresby. And many, many others.

The exhibition broke new ground, not only in this country but also in Europe. Its admirers, however, among them Lynne Thornton in her magnificent volume, *The Orientalists,* and the late Philippe Jullian, often placed it in an 'Orientalist' context with which I have not always agreed. There is room for argument about the use of the term 'Orientalist' when applied to my own collection, which covers a much wider area, both geographical and historical, than is usually covered by 'Orientalism'.

At first I ignored prints, sheered away from books and even set a pre-camera limit of around 1860. But gradually such barriers broke down, thanks largely to John Maggs and the Royal Geographical Society; in both cases my thirst for background knowledge led me to the perusal of their vast stores of illustrated travel books. I became a Fellow of the Royal Geographical Society whose director, Sir Laurence Kirwan, lured me into a thorough search through their store of prints and drawings that had been hidden away in a subterranean catacomb and had never seen the light of day since their acquisition from well-intentioned descendants.

Such exercises widened my knowledge and fields of interest and the collection grew apace, including not merely the work of professional artists but also a multitude of amateurs – soldiers, sailors, architects, archaeologists, etchers, engravers, diplomats and engineers. Some of the less well-known artists were of interest because they covered such wide areas, often off the beaten track and consequently rarely visited by more important artists also represented in the collection. In building up my collection, history and topography caught my interest quite as much as the artistic merit of many of my widely varying quarries. The range developed gradually, extending backwards to early engravings of the sixteenth and seventeenth centuries and forwards, beyond its original limit marked by the advent of the camera, to a growing interest in First World War artists.

With prices at their present level I am tempted to look back on missed opportunities, although any regrets I may harbour on this score are more than compensated by recollection of the excitement

Charlotte Inglefield (d.1901)
Fes Makers at Tunis c.1855-57
Pencil and watercolour, heightened with white; 33.5 x 24.2 cm.
Inscribed; from an album of drawings, *Eastern Sketches.*

of many of the acquisitions that came my way. Two unattributed pencil drawings of Cairo in the collection of a well known dealer were immediately recognisable as being preliminary sketches by David Roberts, one of them for the finished watercolour I have already mentioned (p.68). A hefty album of amateur pencil sketches of incidents relating to the Desert Camel Corps in Wolseley's failed expedition to rescue Gordon in Khartoum in 1885, as well as a number of photographs by a well-known Cairo photographer of that time – again unidentified in the sale catalogue – proved to be by Count Albert Edward Gleichen, Queen Victoria's great-nephew. Frantic research in the day or two available enabled me to identify the album and secure it at the Sotheby sale for £50. Not long afterwards a large batch of amateur watercolours of the same expedition, by a corporal in the Household Cavalry, came to me at a Phillips sale for about £20; not perhaps of great interest to a dealer but of importance in my own particular sphere. Then again a couple of amateurish watercolours at Christie's bore the artist's name, John W. Burgon, whom I remembered as the author of the line 'rose-red city half as old as Time' (Petra). I was the only bidder.

On another occasion I was taken aback by an excellent pencil drawing at Sotheby's, of the ante-room of 'the Pasha' at Cordoba, dated 1833 and confidently attributed to J.F. Lewis. Well, I thought, there were no pashas hanging around in Spain in 1833. An idea sent me rushing home to go through my copy of Lewis's *Illustrations of Constantinople*, all from drawings by Frederick Coke Smyth. And there I found it. It was not Cordoba but Orsova, on the Danube, and 1833 was the right date.

An artist I have been lucky with is Frederick Catherwood (p.31). I originally became interested in him as a result of picking up a vast portfolio of drawings, mostly of Egyptian antiquities, and mostly dating from 1823-24. Several years later I was lucky enough to identify and acquire several unattributed watercolours by Catherwood, which corresponded to the dates of the drawings in this portfolio, or which bore his initials.

Almost unheard of then was Amadeo, fifth Count Preziosi (pp.70 & 135), an artist that I can claim to have helped put back on the map of nineteenth-century painting. His watercolours now command tremendous prices in the sale-rooms. He was immensely prolific, constantly reproducing costume, figure, and street scenes, and was also much copied. He lived for forty years in Constantinople and was a familiar figure in diplomatic and court circles, visited by the Empress Eugénie of France as well as the Prince of Wales, both of whom bought paintings from him; there is a small 'harem' scene in the collection of which the Empress commanded him to make a much larger version.

Another excitement for me was the acquisition at Christie's of an album of sketches by F.C. Lewis Jr, younger brother of J.F. Lewis, who travelled through Turkey on his way to Persia in 1836-37. F.C. nearly came to grief when he set off from Tehran for Bukhara in the company of the unfortunate Colonel Stoddart, who was subsequently murdered in peculiarly horrible circumstances by the notorious Amir of Bukhara. Luckily the British ambassador in Tehran got wind of his protegé's journey and cut short his escapade before he crossed the border, immediately recalling him.

Also relating to this part of the world is a striking watercolour of the terrifying Abdul Samut Khan, by a very good amateur, Godfrey

James McBey (1883-1959)
The First Sight of Jerusalem 1920
Etching and drypoint; 27.7 x 45.8 cm. Signed, inscribed and dated.

Thomas Vigne, who had come across him in Kabul in 1836 (p.100). It caught the eye of the critics at my Leighton House exhibition, which in turn led to a meeting with a Vigne descendant anxious to find a home for two large albums of his sketches in Afghanistan and north-west India. This aim was happily achieved by a partnership between myself and Dr Mildred Archer of the India Office Library. Vigne was a first class amateur draughtsman and explorer, though better at portraits than at landscapes, which were often sketched at great speed and in difficult circumstances. I was later able to pick up several other drawings by him, mostly of Egypt and the Levant, some of which came to light in a wheelbarrow at a country sale in Wales.

There was seldom such good fortune about acquiring works by the big names. These were usually easily recognisable and it was a matter of price, though now and again one slipped through the net. Doubtful attributions to Roberts, were often worth going for, such as one of my Catherwoods, which after unframing and dismounting revealed a date and inscription on the back of the drawing that ruled out Roberts, and pointed clearly to Catherwood. Nor did I despise contemporary copies of Roberts of which there are many and some of which involved me in interesting research.

The only stroke of luck I had with a Lewis was a very dirty Spanish 'lithograph' that I picked up at a country dealer's for a few pounds and that subsequent unframing proved to be an original Lewis watercolour. At that time Lewis's Spanish watercolours were reckoned to be more desirable than his Egyptian works, so I put it into a Sotheby's sale in which there were several other Spanish Lewises but also a typical Lewis Cairo street scene. In the event my Spanish watercolour fetched a price far above what I had to

Henry Thomas Alken (1785-1851)
Two armed figures on horseback, probably Mamluks   1826-30s
Pencil and watercolour, on paper watermarked
J WHATMAN TURKEY MILL 1826; 21.5 x 27.8 cm.

pay, a few lots later, for the street scene that now adorns my collection (p.131).

Archaeological drawings were not always easy to come by as they mostly found their way into museums along with the finds of the artists' employers. But I managed to acquire a large collection of sketches by the young F.C. Cooper, who was working for Layard in Mesopotamia (p.48); desperately homesick and in my opinion much bullied by Layard, he only lasted a year before having to quit because of 'ill health'. Layard himself is also represented in the collection (p.49). Again in the archaeological field, Sir Charles Fellows's successive expeditions to Lycia in south-west Turkey likewise attracted the interest of various artists, both professional and amateur. I found a batch of sketches by the young George Scharf, who accompanied Fellows on two of his Lycian expeditions in 1840 and 1843-44. A great rarity was a pencil sketch, costing me over £90, by the Revd E. T. Daniell, the finished watercolour of which is in the British Museum.

In the architectural field one of my greatest finds was a magnificent album of original drawings by the French architect Pascal Coste, who was employed in Egypt by Muhammad Ali Pasha from 1817 to 1827 (p.84). The album comprises drawings of many of the important Islamic buildings in Cairo. Owen Jones was another of my architectural targets, especially once I acquired the rare volume

of his lithographed Nile views to add to the few original watercolours I already had by him.

Soldiers and sailors had often received training in the art of topography and on the whole are well represented in the collection. Inasmuch as they were apt to find themselves present in circumstances out of reach of professional war artists, their drawings (and the lithographs therefrom) are often of singular interest. The professionals, such as Melton Prior, who covered several military campaigns, were seldom far behind, however, and are also represented in the collection whether by their original sketches or by reference to engravings in, for instance, the *Illustrated London News*. An artist who early caught my special attention was William Simpson (p.24) whose travels took him all over the place, sometimes to current theatres of war, such as the Crimea, sometimes in the company of royal progressions such as the Prince and Princess of Wales's visit to Egypt in 1869. In addition to his publication *Seat of War in the East* (the Crimea), I acquired a number of his original drawings and watercolours, including several sketch-books, which provided a fascinating record of the speed and accuracy of his pencil work – often half a dozen subjects on the same day – of Egypt, Jerusalem and the Crimea (which he revisited after the war).

From time to time artists were hired by travellers or diplomats to record their impressions. Members of the Schranz family of Minorca and Malta, for instance, worked throughout the eastern Mediterranean, often as the hired artist-companions of British travellers who wanted to have a pictorial record of their travels. The father Anton came to Minorca, possibly from Bavaria, around the 1790s, married an English girl by whom he had twelve children, of whom at least three turned out to be competent artists (see pp.40 & 72). The family moved to Malta in 1818. Collectively they were prolific, enjoying the patronage of several British travellers. The third son, Antonio, for example, was employed as Lord Castlereagh's artist-in-residence during his trip through Egypt and the Levant in 1842. The evidence lies in his name being carved, along with the rest of Castlereagh's party (and his dog Dusty), on the exterior of the great Ramesses II temple at Abu Simbel.

Another 'hired' artist who interested me greatly was Luigi Mayer (pp.28 & 37). A great many of his gouache and watercolour drawings were published as coloured aquatints in a series of volumes that are now much sought after. All the books are in my collection along with about a score of his watercolours. Mayer deserves to be regarded as an important forerunner of David Roberts, whose peregrinations he anticipated by some fifty years.

One of the difficulties that I ran into in my early days of collecting was the custom of publishers to have travellers' amateur drawings copied and thereby 'improved' by first-class artists for the purpose of engravings in their popular travel books. Among my early acquisitions was a series of extremely interesting albums of on-the-

Frederick George (active 1860s-1880s)
The Doseh 1885
Grey wash, heightened with white, and with gum; 35.5 x 25.5 cm.
Signed, inscribed and dated.

spot sketches by Mrs Selina Bracebridge, a close friend of Florence
Nightingale. A number of her sketches were 'improved' by such
well-known artists as David Roberts and J.D. Harding for
subsequent engraving and publication in Finden's *Landscape
Illustrations of the Bible*. Her own prowess was such that an album
of her sketches of Turkey in the Victoria and Albert Museum had

been confidently attributed to Edward Lear. The Museum accepted
the correction with good grace.

In principle I excluded works by artists who are not known ever to
have visited the Near or Middle East. There are some notable
exceptions. So greatly did the 'Eastern Question' dominate British
foreign policy during the nineteenth century that I felt justified in
acquiring several of Sir John Tenniel's original drawings for the
cartoons that regularly appeared in *Punch* (p.97). By the same
token, such was the interest and attraction of the Arab horse in
nineteenth-century England that I felt the inclusion of a few works
by (or after) Henry Alken would not be inappropiate (see p.14).

One extraordinary acquisition that came my way consisted of a
group of gouache views of the journey of a Venetian magnate to
Cairo, about 1560-65. They were by an amateur hand (indeed
possibly by two different hands) but my prolonged researches into
the possible identity of the magnate or merchant in question have
so far failed to produce any satisfactory identification or
explanation. I came across them quite by chance at Sotheby's, along
with a few other early but nondescript drawings. There was no bid
for them and I offered £7 for the lot. I spent far more having them
repaired and remounted at the British Museum, where they
aroused great interest, but I reckon them among my prize
acquisitions.

And so the collection continued to grow. Geographically it spread
from the Balkans in the North to Arabia in the South; from North
Africa in the West to Persia and Afghanistan in the East.
Chronologically there is very little earlier than the mid-sixteenth
century and not much later than the early twentieth century. Most
of the artists represented are British but the collection also includes
French, Italian, German, Swiss, Scandinavian, Spanish, Dutch,
Russian, and even one or two American artists.

As the collection expanded so did interest in it increase, aided by
exposure through several exhibitions, illustrations in books and
even a television programme. The problem of finding a permanent
home for it became pressing. Various friends who had followed
and indeed assisted in its development were determined that it
should be preserved intact, for the benefit of future generations.

I laid down certain criteria for its disposal: namely that it should
remain in the UK, and that it should be accessible to the public. The
Victoria and Albert Museum was able to promise to preserve its
separate identity and to have it systematically catalogued. I hope
that those who contributed to the Museum's purchase of the
collection – my old employers Shell, the Italian fashion designer
Gianni Versace, the National Heritage Memorial Fund, the
National Art-Collections Fund, and the Friends of the V&A – will
see from this book and the exhibition it accompanies that they made
a wise investment for posterity. Posterity has also been blessed
with a comprehensive illustrated catalogue of the entire collection,

available on COMfiche. For this I must pay the highest tribute to the staff of the Prints and Drawings Department of the Museum, notably Michael Kauffman (now Director of the Courtauld Institute of Art), and Charles Newton, who has overseen the cataloguing; also to Michael Darby, whose interest in the collection was instrumental in the Museum's acquisition of it; and to the team of cataloguers – Briony Llewellyn, who has devoted enormous amounts of time and patience to it over several years, Tanya Szrajber and Jenny Elkan. Between them they have converted my voluminous and often highly imaginative notes into a most scholarly documentation, thus greatly enhancing the usefulness of the collection not only to students but also, I hope, to the general public.

And although I have indeed found separation from the collection and all that it involved in my life a sad wrench, I have the great satisfaction of knowing that it has found in the V&A an ideal home.

Rodney Searight

Lewis Vulliamy (1791-1871)
Şehzade Camii, Constantinople c.1818
Pencil, on paper watermarked *J GREEN 1813*; 26.4 x 42 cm.

WEST FINDS EAST
Scholars, travellers and tourists

For centuries the Orient has exerted a powerful fascination over the West. The lands between North Africa and India, with their widely differing peoples, architecture and landscape, but linked by their Islamic culture, have drawn travellers from Europe for reasons as various as trade, politics, religion, art and antiquity, and plain curiosity.

The remains of ancient civilisations that lie scattered throughout the region have been – and remain – one of its special attractions. From the mid-eighteenth century on they were gradually rediscovered and systematically surveyed by western scholars, explorers and archaeologists: Palmyra and Baalbek in the 1750s, the great cities of Asia Minor in the later eighteenth and early nineteenth centuries, Petra in 1812, the cities of Assyria in the 1840s, and the temples and tombs of Pharaonic Egypt throughout the nineteenth century.

As these sites became better known to the European public, and with travel facilitated by the development of steam transport, the numbers of visitors to them increased, to include not just the wealthy dilettante or hardy explorer but the interested tourist as well. By the middle decades of the nineteenth century, tourism in the Near East was well established. In Egypt, for example, it could be a leisurely affair, undertaken by individuals such as the unidentified traveller, 'J.W.P.', whose Nile boat is seen in the watercolour by Émile Prisse d'Avennes (p.23), or it could be a rush past the ruins on a runaway donkey, as William Simpson's tongue-in-cheek watercolour encapsulates (p.25). The Overland Route, fully established in the late 1840s for travellers between Europe and India, brought many visitors to Egypt, even if it was for only a few hours' sightseeing in Cairo and a mad dash across the desert to or from Suez in a vehicle such as the coach and four portrayed by Count Andrassy (p.26).

after Gavin Hamilton (1723-1798)

James Dawkins and Robert Wood Esqrs, First discovering Sight of Palmyra.   1773-75

Etching and engraving, by John Hall (1739-1797)
Cut to 44.2 x 53 cm.
Lettered with title and *Painted by G. Hamilton 1758. Engraved by John Hall 1773 Published May 12th 1775, by J.Robson, New Bond Street.*
From an original picture in the Possession of Henry Dawkins Esqr.

In 1751 Robert Wood and James Dawkins, assisted by the Italian artist Giovanni Battista Borra, made the first systematic survey of the classical ruins at Palmyra and Baalbek. Their subsequent publications, *Ruins of Palmyra* (1753; see p.43) and *Ruins of Balbec* (1757), were immensely influential in Britain, creating a surge in the taste for the Neo-Classical style in architecture as well as in the scientific investigation of ancient ruins.

In 1758 their achievement was celebrated in a painting (currently on loan to Glasgow University) by Gavin Hamilton, a Scottish artist, who was also notable as an archaeologist and a dealer. He spent most of his extremely successful career in Rome, but, through his British contacts, he also played an important part in the rise of Neo-Classicism in Britain. His painting, reproduced in this print, shows Wood and Dawkins arriving at Palmyra, with Borra (turbaned and holding a drawing), and their Arab escort. In contrast to Pars's almost contemporary interpretation of a similar event (see p.20), Hamilton has made no attempt to depict the arrival realistically; instead he proclaims its significance by portraying the explorers as classical heroes, dressed in Roman togas. Their Arab guards, in voluminous cloaks and elaborate turbans, are also suitably dignified, and although, according to reports, armed to the teeth, only one long pike is visible. A token palm tree adds oriental flavour, but the artist's primary intention has been to pay an appropriately classical tribute to the explorers' momentous discovery.

after William Pars (1742-1782)

The Theatre at Miletus 1780

Etching and aquatint, by Paul Sandby (1730-1809)
32.8 x 51.3 cm.
Lettered *MILETUS   P Sandby F   W Pars Pinx   Published by P Sandby*
St Georges Row Oxford Turnpik January 1st 1780.

Inspired by the example of Wood and Dawkins (p.18), the Society of Dilettanti (a group of noblemen and gentlemen, founded in 1733, one of whose aims was to further the appreciation of the antique) sponsored several expeditions to Greece and Asia Minor to examine classical sites. One of these was led by Richard Chandler, accompanied by Pars, a topographical artist, and Nicholas Revett, an architect, and in 1764-65 they visited several of the Greco-Roman sites in western Turkey.

Here the three English travellers, accompanied by their Turkish guides, are seen crossing the river Maeander on a raft in order to see the antiquities of Miletos, the greatest city of ancient Ionia. Chandler was not impressed by the ruins except for the theatre,

'visible afar off and ... a most capacious edifice'. Pars reflects this opinion in his distant view of the site, where only the theatre is prominent, focussing attention instead on the throng of men and horses in the foreground, and on the contrast between the dress and demeanour of the English tourists and that of the local inhabitants.

Sandby's set of eleven (possibly twelve) aquatints from Pars's watercolours (now in the British Museum), were completed between about 1777 and 1780 and were among the earliest aquatints to appear in Britain. Pars's watercolours were also published as engravings in Chandler's *Ionian Antiquities* (Vol.1, 1769; Vol.2, 1797).

Michel-François Préaulx (active 1787-1827)

The Gardens of the Seraglio with European
Visitors inspecting the Column of the
Goths, Constantinople   c.1800-20

Pen and ink and watercolour
39.2 x 57.8 cm.

This watercolour, and the one by Denon (p.22), belong to a long-established tradition of images showing artists and scholars drawing, measuring and otherwise observing ancient monuments. While Préaulx sketches in the foreground, one of his patrons is examining the Goth's Column, a granite monolith fifteen metres high, surmounted by a Corinthian capital. Dating from the third or fourth century AD, it is one of the oldest but least known monuments in the city. It stands in what is now Gülhane Park, between Topkapı Sarayı and Saray Burnu (Seraglio Point).

Préaulx arrived in Constantinople in 1796 with a group of fellow French architects and artists, commissioned to provide military and naval installations for the Ottoman administration, governed by the westward-looking Sultan, Selim III (see p.94). The artist survived the strain in relations between France and Turkey provoked by the Napoleonic Wars, and continued to execute topographical drawings for many British and French visitors, including Lord Elgin, British Ambassador in Constantinople, 1799-1803.

21

Baron Dominique Vivant Denon (1747-1825)

Vue de la colonne de Pompée à Alexandrie 1798

Watercolour over pencil, on laid paper watermarked *D & C BLAUW*
21.2 x 26.8 cm.
Numbered *44*; inscribed on the back with title

Napeoleon's invasion of Egypt in 1798 was far reaching in its consequences, not so much strategic, since his military campaign ended with a whimper, as cultural. From then on Egypt, both ancient and modern, was a subject of considerable interest for the West: western influences pervaded various aspects of Egyptian life and, as a result of western scrutiny, Egyptian culture made its own impact on European civilisation.

These repercussions were set off by the large group of *savants* (scholars and experts in a variety of fields) that Napoleon brought with him, and whose brief was to study all aspects of Egyptian life and history, past and present. Here some of them are seen measuring the height of Pompey's Column by flying a kite, watched by two men in the right foreground who have arrived on horseback – possibly Napoleon and the artist. The red granite column, twenty-two metres high and crowned by an immense capital, was raised in AD300 in honour of the Emperor Diocletian. Its name derives from the mistaken medieval belief that it marked the site of the temple built in honour of Pompey.

Baron Denon was one of the most eminent intellectuals of his day. His career reflected the diversity of his interests: he was an Egyptologist, an artist, an author and an antiquarian, as well as a courtier at Versailles, a diplomat, and the first Director of the Louvre. He accompanied Napoleon to Egypt, but remained independent of the Institut d'Égypte and published his own account of the country, *Voyage dans la Basse et la Haute Égypte* in 1802, well in advance of the official and much larger *Description de L'Égypte* (20 vols, 1809-22).

Achille-Constant-Théodore-Émile Prisse d'Avennes (1807-1879)

A *Kanja* on the Nile at Luxor   c.1838-43

Watercolour, formerly laid down on card watermarked *J WHATMAN 1839[?]*
25.1 x 33.7 cm.
Inscribed on the back of the old mount *My Boat on the Nile   J.W.P.*
By Prise.

Artist, writer, linguist, traveller, archaeologist and engineer, Prisse d'Avennes was one of those versatile and colourful characters who enliven the history of the nineteenth century. Like his fellow countrymen, Coste and Linant de Bellefonds (pp.84 & 30), his skills were employed by Muhammad Ali to assist in the modernisation of Egypt, but his impatience with authority soon caused him to strike out on his own. In the late 1830s and early 1840s he acquired a reputation among European travellers for his knowledge of, and skill in copying the inscriptions and reliefs in the ancient temples and tombs at Thebes (Luxor), as well as for his more individual and lively topographical views (see also p.118). The watercolour shown here was one of many commissions that Prisse received, in this case

from an unidentified British tourist, 'J.W.P.', who flew a Red Ensign at the stern of his hired *kanja*. The boat is moored beside the east bank of the Nile on the other side of which is an island, Gazirat Saad, and behind this a hill, Gabal Qurnat; between the palm trees can just be discerned the Colossi of Memnon.

When Prisse returned to France in 1844 he furthered his reputation as an Egyptologist with several publications, including the monumental and lavishly illustrated *L'Histoire de l'Art Egyptien* (3 vols, 1858-77). In addition, during a return visit to Egypt in 1858-60, he devoted himself to the serious study of its Islamic culture, which culminated in another sumptuous publication, *L'Art Arabe* (4 vols, 1869-77).

William Simpson RI FRGS (1823-1899)

Heliopolis – As It Is   1878

Pencil, watercolour and bodycolour, heightened with white
37.3 x 26.5 cm.
Inscribed with title, signed and dated *Wm. Simpson. 1878*

Simpson is here making a wry comment on the growth of tourism
in Egypt. The two tourists, engrossed in maintaining their seat on
the galloping donkeys, have apparently failed to notice an ancient
Egyptian monument, despite the attempts of a local youth to attract
their attention. Also unregarded are the native inhabitants, riding
on camels rather more sedately. In the middle stands the obelisk,
oldest of all, sole survivor of the ancient cult city of On, or
Heliopolis, and indifferent to human idiosyncrasy. The trippers
may well have been taking part in a Cook's tour, by then fast
becoming a regular feature of Egyptian tourism, bringing the
celebrated monuments within the reach of ordinary people (some
of whom, according to Simpson, failed to appreciate them).

Simpson acquired fame as 'Crimean' Simpson, from his
illustrations of the Crimean War, published as *The Seat of War in the
East* (1855-56). In 1866 he became the first of the 'Special Artists'
employed by the *Illustrated London News* to report on and illustrate
the military confrontations and grand ceremonial occasions
undertaken by the British Empire. Among several royal tours that
he accompanied was the visit of the Prince and Princess of Wales
to Egypt in 1869, a few months before the official opening of the
Suez Canal (see p.96). A pencil drawing in a sketch-book from this
trip (also in the Searight Collection) shows this obelisk, later to be
the subject of the watercolour seen here. Simpson himself had
travelled through the Canal when he journeyed round the world
in 1872-73.

Heliopolis.—Bj st of. Wm Simpson. 1878.

after Count Mano Andrassy (1821-1891)

Habitation Arabe Dans La Plaine De Suez   1859

Colour lithograph, by Eugène Ciceri (1813-1890) and Victor Adam
(1801-1866), with additional colouring by hand
29.7 x 44.5 cm.
Lettered *Aegyptom* and with title in Czech and French, and *Cte. Andrasi
del.   Eug. Ciceri et. V.Adam lith.   Imp. Lemercier, Paris.*

A party of well-to-do travellers are seen crossing the desert between
Suez and Cairo on the short overland section of the route between
India and Europe via the Red Sea, before the Suez Canal connecting
the Red Sea with the Mediterranean had been built. In the distance
on the left can be seen one of the semaphore towers set up to send
messages along the route. Oblivious to the march of modern
progress are three camels, representing more traditional means
of travel, and an Arab dwelling, where life continues as it has
always done.

Andrassy was a Czech industrialist whose extensive travels
included a visit to India and China via this so-called Overland
Route. He subsequently published an account of his journey, in
Czech in 1853 and in German in 1859, as *Reise des Grafen Emanuel
Andrasy in Ostindien, Ceylon, Java, China und Bengalien*, in which
26   this lithograph appeared as a plate.

ANTIQUITIES
Egyptian and Classical

'. . . forth suddenly came the Rameses Heads!! I was absolutely too astonished and affected to draw . . . As a whole the scene is overpowering from its beauty – colour – solitude – history – art – poetry – every sort of association . . . all other visible things in this world seem to be as chips, or potatoparings, or any nonsense in comparison.' Such was Edward Lear's response to the Temple of Ramesses II at Abu Simbel when he saw it in 1867, half a century after it had first been examined and excavated (see p.30).

At different times the diverse antiquities of the Near East have elicited a variety of visual responses from artists. These have included careful delineations of the architectural and decorative features of the ruins, as well as less accurate but more vivid views of certain sites, deliberately composed to create a particular pictorial effect. The early nineteenth-century rules of picturesque composition demanded that ruins should be depicted in a landscape setting with appropriate local figures, or 'staffage', to enliven the scene, as, for example, in the watercolours by Bartlett and Schranz (pp.46 & 40). From the 1840s on, however, artists like William Müller and Carl Haag (pp.41 & 42) sometimes dispensed with this tradition and focussed on the aesthetic aspects of a ruin in its environment.

Luigi Mayer FSA (c.1750-1803)

View of Grand Cairo from the Summit of the Great Pyramid of Giza   c.1800

Watercolour and gouache with gum, heightened with white,
on paper watermarked *J WHATMAN 1794*
54.6 x 90.7 cm.
Lettered *VEDUTA DEL GRAN CAIRO CON LI SUOI SOBBORGHI DA BULAK FINO A SACCARA PRESA DALLA SOMMITA DELLA MAGGIORE PIRAMIDE DI GIZA.*
and signed *L. Mayer dipinse*

With its considerable size and unusual viewpoint, this is one of Mayer's most impressive watercolours. The contrast between the large figures standing on the vast cut blocks of the ancient Egyptian Pyramid and the barren, featureless desert, with the outline of modern Cairo in the distance, is startling.

Mayer was one of the earliest professional artists to travel in Egypt: he probably went there in 1792, six years before Napoleon's expedition brought the country to the attention of the West. He trained as an artist in Rome, and after working in Naples was employed as draughtsman by Sir Robert Ainslie during his tenure as British Ambassador in Constantinople, 1776-94. During this time Mayer travelled throughout the Ottoman Empire drawing its antiquities, landscape and people. He accompanied Ainslie back to England and published several volumes of 'views' in Turkey, Syria, Palestine, Egypt, and Cyprus (see p.37). The first, *Views in Egypt* (1801-04), provided the British public with illustrations of many of the antiquities of Lower Egypt, more than forty years before the publication of David Roberts's better-known *Egypt & Nubia* (1846-49). One of the aquatints in Mayer's *Egypt* reproduces, in a reduced version, the view seen here.

attributed to
Louis Maurice Adolphe Linant de Bellefonds, Bey and Pasha (1799-1883)

Excavation of the Great Temple of Ramesses II
at Abu Simbel   Probably 1818-19

Watercolour over pencil, on paper watermarked *[J WHA]TMAN [TURKEY]
MILL [...]6*
17.1 x 23.9 cm.

An intrepid and versatile Frenchman, Linant came to Egypt in 1818. In Cairo he adopted the life of an Ottoman Turk, but was known and consulted by European residents and visitors as well as by the Pasha of Egypt, Muhammad Ali. At various times his talents were employed as a geographer, explorer, engineer, cartographer and draughtsman.

His first adventure was an expedition to Upper Egypt that Henry Salt, British Consul-General in Egypt (see p.54), took to Abu Simbel in 1818-19. Although there were other artists in the party it is likely that this watercolour is by Linant and that it depicts Salt's attempts to clear away the ever encroaching sand from the façade of the Great Temple. It shows the construction of a palisade of date-palm trunks to keep back the sand, held in place by wet mud brought up from the Nile in sacks by the local villagers.

Linant took part in several subsequent expeditions up the Nile, and was one of the first Europeans to reach the Pharaonic sites of Meroe and Musawarat in the Sudan. Later, he played a prominent part in irrigation projects in Lower Egypt and in plans for the Suez Canal.

Frederick Catherwood (1799-1854)

Temple of Sabua, Nubia   1824

Pencil and watercolour, heightened with white, on grey-buff paper
25.8 x 36.7 cm.
Numbered *18*; inscribed and dated on the back *Temple of Sebooa – Nubia*
Feby 10th

This drawing depicts the partly rock-cut Temple of Ramesses II at Sabua, which, when Lake Nasser was created in the 1960s, was moved four kilometers to the west of its original site.

Catherwood was a well-travelled architectural and topographical draughtsman, and later a railway engineer. This is one of many drawings made during his first visit to Egypt, in 1823-24, in the company of Henry Westcar, a wealthy gentleman traveller, and two other architects, Henry Parke and Joseph John Scoles. Westcar's diary of their journey up the Nile to Wadi Halfa and back to Cairo recounts their adventures with youthful gusto. The Searight Collection also contains a large group of sketches made by

Catherwood, and possibly his companions, with the assistance of a *camera lucida*, a drawing aid incorporating a prism through which the outline of an image is reflected on to the paper.

Catherwood returned to Egypt in 1832 to assist in excavations directed by Robert Hay of Linplum, and in 1833 he joined fellow artists, Francis Arundale and Joseph Bonomi, on a journey across Sinai to Jerusalem and on to Syria and Lebanon. In London his watercolours were used to make large panoramas. Between 1839 and 1842 he twice visited Central America with the explorer John Lloyd Stephens.

Captain Charles Francklin Head (1796-1849)

The Ramesseum: Mortuary Temple of Ramesses II, Luxor   1830-33

Brown wash over pencil, on stiff paper
27.5 x 41.2 cm.
Inscribed on the back *Thebes*

Captain Head was an officer in the Queen's Royal Regiment. After serving in India he travelled home to England through Egypt using a detour on what later became the well-trodden Overland Route. Arriving in Qusayr from Jiddah and Bombay on 28 December 1829, he crossed the desert to the Nile, visited Thebes (Luxor), and travelled on down river, reaching Alexandria on 18 February 1830. On his return to England he published *Eastern and Egyptian Scenery, Ruins, &c* (1833), a series of lithographs after his own sketches that showed the celebrated monuments accessible from the Overland Route. The Searight Collection contains five of these original sketches, including the one here for Plate 8, published with the title *Ruins of the Memnonium, with Part of the Cemetery of Thebes*.

The temple's nineteenth-century name derived from the erroneous identification of its colossal statue with the Trojan hero Memnon. The statue in fact represents the Eighteenth Dynasty Pharaoh, Ramesses II, venerated in this temple. The head of another statue of the Pharaoh is seen in this view; its companion, removed from the site by Belzoni in 1816 (see below), inspired Shelley's poem, *Ozymandias* (1818). On the right are the Osiris columns of the first court of the temple.

after Giovanni Battista Belzoni (1778-1823)

Seti I being conducted by Horus into the presence of Osiris   1820

Copy of a painted low-relief from the south wall of the first pillared hall in the Tomb of Seti I, Valley of the Kings, Thebes
Lithograph, by Charles-Joseph Hullmandel (1789-1850), coloured by hand
53.8 x 44.3 cm.
Lettered *FROM THE TOMBS OF THE KINGS AT THEBES: DISCOVERED BY G.BELZONI* and *London. Published by J.Murray 1820.   C.Hullmandel's Lithography;* also *Plate 19* and *Belzoni del*

Belzoni's discovery of the Tomb of Seti I in October 1817 was but one of his remarkable exploits in Egypt. Working for Henry Salt (see p.30 & 54) between 1815 and 1819, he had removed the head of the 'Young Memnon' from its site at Thebes (Luxor) (see above) and transported it back to London, along with many other antiquities; cleared away the sand from the façade and entered the Great Temple at Abu Simbel; found the entrance to the Second Pyramid at Giza; and discovered six royal tombs in the Valley of the Kings, including that of Seti I.

Everything that Belzoni did seemed to be larger than life; earlier, his exceptional physique had brought him fame as a performing 'strong man'. Never one to miss his place in the limelight, he published in 1820 his spectacular discoveries in Egypt, in his *Narrative Of The Researches And Operations Of G.Belzoni In Egypt And Nubia*, with an accompanying volume of coloured *Plates*, of which the lithograph illustrated here is one. The success of these publications prompted him to open an exhibition in Piccadilly the following year of Egyptian antiquities and copies of tomb paintings, including full-sized replicas of two of the chambers in Seti I's tomb. This caused a sensation and attracted thousands of visitors during its year-long run. Not until Howard Carter (see p.34) discovered the Tomb of Tutankhamun a century later did an archaeologist in Egypt achieve such widespread fame.

FROM THE TOMBS OF THE KINGS AT THEBES, DISCOVERED BY G. BELZONI.

London. Published by J. Murray 1820.

33

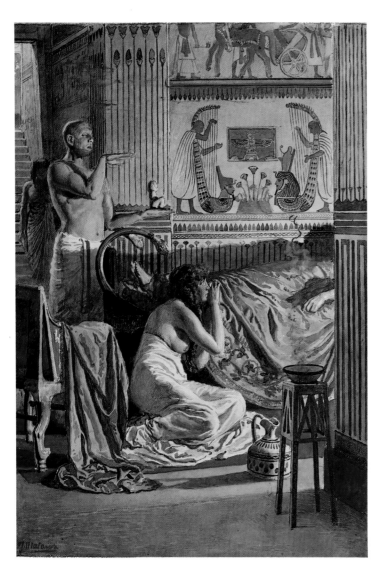

Fortunino Matania RI (1881-1963)

The Exorcist   1923

Watercolour and gouache, over pencil, on board
40.1 x 27.3 cm.
Signed *F.Matania*; on the back, inscribed in another hand with title (twice), artist's name and printers' notes, stamped and numbered THE SPHERE No1.205; in the margins, inscribed with further printers' notes

One of the many ways in which Howard Carter's discovery of Tutankhamun's tomb caught popular imagination is illustrated in this fanciful interpretation of the death of an Egyptian Pharaoh, made for a special Egyptian section of *The Sphere* magazine for 24 February 1923. Entitled *Pharaoh Falls Ill – The Exorcist is called in*, it was the first of four equally far-fetched illustrations depicting the last journey of a pharaoh from his palace to his tomb. The necromancer has been summoned to drive away the evil spirit possessing the body of the sick ruler, but the charms he holds out and the incantations he utters are to no avail, and the pharaoh dies.

Matania was an Italian illustrator and historical painter, described in the introduction to this Egyptian section in the magazine as having 'a very special genius for reconstructing the past'. He was *The Sphere*'s Special Artist, and also worked for other periodicals in Milan, Paris and London.

Howard Carter (1874-1939)

Head of Queen Makare Hatshepsut   1893-1906

Copy of a painted low relief in the Mortuary Temple of Hatshepsut, Deir al-Bahri
Watercolour, heightened with white
54.5 x 47.5 cm.
Signed *Howard Carter*

Carter began excavating in Egypt thirty years before his famous discovery in 1922 of the Tomb of Tutankhamun in the Valley of the Kings. One of his earliest assignments was as draughtsman accompanying the investigations of the Swiss archaeologist, Henri Edouard Naville, at the Temple of Hatshepsut at Deir al-Bahri. Between 1893 and 1899 Carter made copies of all the visible wall paintings and inscriptions, and these were later photographically reproduced in Naville's six folio volumes, *The Temple of Deir el Bahari* (1895-1908).

This watercolour is a copy of one of the few representations of Queen Hatshepsut (who reigned as a pharaoh of the Eighteenth Dynasty, 1503-1482 BC) to survive defacement by her successor. Her portrait is a detail of the scene, *Offering of Vases to Amon*, which is Plate CXXXI of Part V in Naville's publication.

Louis François Cassas (1756-1827)

View of the Theatre of Myra, Asia Minor   1808

Ink and watercolour, on paper watermarked *J.RUSE 1806*
57 x 77.8 cm.
Signed and dated *L.F.Cassas f. 1808.*; on the back inscribed *[Vu]e du Theatre De Cacanie en Caramancie,* and on two labels attached to the back of the frame, inscribed similarly and *24. Vue prise sue la côte de L'Asie Mineure, par Cassas.*

Cassas was a skilled draughtsman and painter of picturesque landscapes and figure subjects. After his training in France he spent five years in Italy. In September 1784 he arrived in Constantinople with the comte de Choiseul-Gouffier, the French Ambassador to the Ottoman Empire, and a month later embarked on a long journey to Syria, Lebanon, Palestine, Cyprus and Egypt, returning in January 1786. After another expedition to Asia Minor, Greece and its islands, he returned to Rome in 1787 and many years later some of his drawings were engraved for publication in his *Voyage pittoresque de la Syrie, de la Phénicie, de la Palestine et de la Basse-Égypte* (1799).

Although the ruins represented in this watercolour are recognisable as the theatre and tombs of ancient Myra in Lycia (modern Demre, on the south-west coast of Turkey), their situation in a fertile landscape with lush vegetation and a waterfall fed from the lake behind is fanciful. In this, as in similarly elaborate watercolours of ruins at Ephesus or Baalbek painted many years after his direct experience of them, Cassas's concern was to convey the romantic atmosphere of the place rather than accurately to delineate its topography. A more prosaic view of the same place is seen in Luigi Mayer's nearly contemporaneous *View of the Theatre at Myra* (p.37).

Luigi Mayer FSA (c.1750-1803)

View of the Theatre at Myra c.1797

Watercolour and gouache, with gum, on laid paper
watermarked *I. HONIG*
42 x 56.5 cm.
Lettered *VEDUTA INTERIORE DEL TEATRO NEL TERRIO DI CACCAMO,*
LA SCENA DI ORDINE COMPOSITO CON COLONNE DI GRANITO GRIGIO

This view of the theatre, produced for an English patron, contrasts
with Cassas's romanticised interpretation of the scene (p.36),
which caters for a more elaborate, French taste. The prominent
figure in the foreground, seen from the back, is nevertheless a
deliberate artifice, introduced by Mayer both to draw the viewer's
eye into the picture and to emphasise the oriental context of the
subject. Versions of the view were reproduced in the Society of
Dilettanti's *Antiquities of Ionia* (Part 2, 1797, Pl.LVII), and in Mayer's
Views in the Ottoman Empire (1803, Pl.5). (See also p.28.)

Caccamo was the Italian name for the area of coast and islands in
south-west Turkey between and including Myra and Patara, in
which there were several ancient ruins.

John Peter Gandy RA (afterwards Deering) (1787-1850)

A Tomb in Lycia, Turkey
Probably 1812-13

Watercolour over pencil, on stiff paper
14.1 x 25.3 cm.
Inscribed on former mount *J.P.Gandy.*

Gandy was an architect and draughtsman. In 1811-13 he took part in an expedition led by Sir William Gell, on behalf of the Society of Dilettanti, that investigated and drew antiquities in Greece and south-west Turkey, including Lycia. A large number of drawings from the trip are in the collections of the Royal Institute of British Architects. The watercolour shown here was probably done shortly after that trip, but it has not yet been possible to identify the tomb, despite the distinctive relief on its side. It may have been destroyed, or Gandy may even have concocted the tomb from various sources, and placed it in a suitably picturesque setting.

Clarkson Frederick Stanfield RA (1793-1867)

Sardis   1834-35

Watercolour and bodycolour, heightened with white, over pencil, and with scratching out, on stiff paper
23.3 x 35.3 cm.

Sardis was the capital of the ancient kingdom of Lydia. It prospered during the Hellenistic, Roman and Byzantine periods and was an important early Christian bishopric, one of the Seven Churches of *Revelations*. The two Ionic columns of the Temple of Artemis are the most impressive remains of the ancient city. Stanfield did not visit the site (or anywhere in the Near East), but based his composition on a sketch by an amateur artist, Maude (see opposite). He has totally transformed Maude's unsophisticated composition by setting the two columns against a stormy sky rent by lightning and introducing the foreground drama of frightened horse and unseated rider. The scene has become a vehicle for a restatement of the popular romantic theme of feeble man overwhelmed by the

elements while ancient stones stand unmoved.

Stanfield was a well-known painter in oils and watercolours, mainly of landscapes and marine views. Among the several publications to which he contributed was *Landscape Illustrations of the Bible*, published by the Finden brothers in 1836. His watercolour of Sardis was engraved by William Finden for Vol.2.

possibly by – Maude (active c.1830-36)

Sardis c.1830-35

Brown wash over pencil, on paper watermarked WHATMAN *1829*
24.9 x 29.4 cm.
Inscribed on mount with title

This is probably the original sketch by — *Maude, Esq.* that Clarkson Stanfield redrew for the engraving by W.Finden in T.H.Horne's *Landscape Illustrations of the Bible*, published by the Finden brothers in 1836. Maude was a little known amateur artist who travelled in Greece and Asia Minor in the early 1830s.

Antonio Schranz (1801-after 1865)

View of the Ruins and Hot Springs at Pamukkale 1837

Watercolour over pencil
34 x 51 cm.
On the back numbered *40*, signed with initials A.S., inscribed *Hierapolis – Natural Hot Spring. Phrygia.* and dated *Janry 8th 1837*

Schranz was one of a family of topographical artists based in Malta. Between 1823 and 1847 he made at least ten journeys to the Near East, often accompanying British travellers as their draughtsman. This watercolour, along with fifteen others in the Searight Collection, resulted from one such journey, made in 1836-37 with an unidentified patron. Schranz's generalised treatment of the ancient ruins of Hierapolis makes them less the focus of attention than their natural surroundings, enlivened by the touches of contemporary local colour provided by the bathers and onlookers. The result is a picturesque view not far in spirit from the picture postcards of today.

William James Müller (1812-1845)

Ruins at Tlos, Lycia   1844

Watercolour over pencil
32.2 x 53.5 cm.
Inscribed *Tlos*, dated and signed with initials *Janr. 8. 1844. WM*

Müller pursued an active career as a painter of landscapes and
genre subjects, but his ambitions were cut short by his early death.
While he achieved fame as a rapid and fluent watercolour sketcher,
he was disappointed by his failure to find recognition as an oil
painter. He travelled to the Near East twice in search of new and
exotic subjects, first to Egypt in 1838-39, and later, in 1843-44, to
south-west Turkey, where he drew the people, the scenery and the
ancient remains of Lycia.

In this watercolour Müller has focussed on the Roman arches on
the eastern face of the rocky crag occupied by the acropolis of the
Lycian city of Tlos. The ruins are seen as part of the rugged mountain
scenery, which he has depicted with subtly varying tints of earthy
colours applied with broad sweeps of his brush, leaving areas of
white paper to convey the transparent elements of light and air.

Carl Haag RWS (1820-1915)

The Triumphal Arch, Palmyra   1859

Watercolour, with scraping out, on thick paper
30 x 60.5 cm.
Inscribed with title, signed and dated *Carl Haag Sept. 1859.;*
inscribed on the back *The Triumphal Arch in Palmyra   East View.*
and signed and dated *Carl Haag 1859.*

'If I am a ruined man all my life, or if I walk there in Bedouin sandals, I *must go* to Palmyra!' This, according to Emily Beaufort, was Haag's reaction on seeing sketches of the ruins. When they reached them in October 1859 they were not disappointed. Emily Beaufort's book, *Egyptian Sepulchres and Syrian Shrines* (1861), describes them eulogistically and at length; Haag made several sketches, which became the basis of watercolours exhibited in London on his return. In their preoccupation with the light and atmosphere of the site, these watercolours are very different from the dry, academic plans and architectural details published a century earlier in Robert Wood's *Ruins of Palmyra* (1753; see p.43).

Haag's trip to Palmyra was part of an extended visit to Egypt, Palestine, Syria and Lebanon lasting fifteen months in 1858-60. He was a prolific and successful painter in watercolours, and after this journey specialised in oriental subjects (see p.126). Born in Bavaria, he came to London in 1847 and by 1850 had evolved an elaborate watercolour technique which, as he affirmed, achieved the 'brilliancy of oil painting, combined with the tender-sweetness of water-colours'.

After their 'rediscovery' for the West by Wood and Dawkins in the mid-eighteenth century (see p 18) Palmyra's ruins became famous for their beauty and for their isolated position in the Syrian desert. Only the most intrepid travellers, however, braved the arduous and hazardous trek across the sands. The city had flourished in the first to the third centuries AD from its location on one of the major trade routes between Rome and the East. Most of its great monuments were built at this time, including the Triumphal Arch in the second century, as the gateway to the colonnaded street.

after Giovanni Battista Borra (1712-1786)

The Triumphal Arch, Palmyra   1753

Etching, by Johann Sebastian Müller (1715-1785)
23.5 x 36.4 cm.
Lettered *Tab: XXVI* and *J.P.Borra Arch: del: J.B.Müller sc:*

Plate XXVI from Robert Wood, *The Ruins of Palmyra, Otherwise Tedmor, In The Desert* (1753; see p.18). The volume consists of fifty-seven plates after drawings by Borra, an Italian artist and architect.

William Edward Dighton (1822-1853)

Temple of Bacchus, Baalbek   1852-53

Pencil and watercolour
35.5 x 52.5 cm.

Dighton was a watercolour painter of landscapes, from Bristol. His
work has often been attributed to W.J. Müller (see p.41), who was
his friend and mentor. His only recorded visit to the Near East was
a tour of Egypt, Sinai, Palestine and Lebanon in 1852, shortly before
his early death. His watercolours from this trip, six of which are in
the Searight Collection, show his preoccupation with the light and
colour of the landscape. In the example here the temple is
inseparable from its hot dry environment; its architectural details
are almost obliterated by the brightness of the pervading sunlight.

Lauret
either Emmanuel-Joseph Lauret
(known as Lauret Aîné) (1809-1882)
or François Lauret (1820-1868)

The Praetorium at Lambesa, Algeria
Probably 1853

Watercolour and bodycolour, heightened with white, over pencil, on paper watermarked *J WHATM[AN] TURKEY MII[I] 184[...]*
46.9 x 59.4 cm.
Signed and incorrectly dated *Lauret 1833*, and inscribed *Lambèse*; inscribed on the back *Praetorium Lambessa*

Emmanuel-Joseph and François Lauret were brothers, both based in Toulon painting landscapes and rural scenes, and both living and working at various times in Algeria. Lauret Aîné was there in 1850-62, his brother joining him in 1851-54, and again in 1860-66. Another watercolour (also in the Searight Collection) of the gorge of Al Cantara, not far from Lambesa, is signed and dated *Lauret ainé 1853*. It appears to be by the same hand, but it is not impossible that François Lauret was working in a very similar style.

The Praetorium at Lambesa is one of the finest Roman buildings in Africa. The town was founded as an army camp and in the second century AD became the headquarters of the Third Augustan Legion, whose responsibility was the defence of North Africa. The Praetorium was the residence of the Roman military commander.

William Henry Bartlett (1809-1854)

Principal Range of Tombs, Petra   1845-48

Ink, watercolour and bodycolour, heightened with white, over pencil
22.3 x 35.9 cm.
Inscribed *Petra* and with note to the engraver; inscribed on the back
with title

Bartlett was a prolific topographical artist who travelled extensively
in search of new and interesting subjects for his drawings. He
visited North Africa and the Near East seven times, and made
several other trips in Britain and Europe, as well as North America.
Popular demand for travel books was high during the 1830s and
1840s, and Bartlett contributed illustrations to several of them,
including about a dozen written by himself.

This watercolour resulted from his visit to Petra in November 1845,
which he reached from Aqaba, having crossed Sinai from Cairo. It
was engraved for Bartlett's account of his journey, *Forty Days in the
Desert* (1848; facing p.134, by J.Cousen). The 'marvellous and
romantic singularity of this wonderful region', as Bartlett described

Petra in his book, inspired an unusually detailed watercolour that
shows well his habitual use of pale coloured washes for the
landscape, with ink outlines and denser pigment to give emphasis
to the figures.

The view includes the Corinthian Tomb and other large and well-
preserved tombs on the eastern side of the valley; on the right can
be seen the Wadi Musa, with, in the distance, the outline of the
theatre.

Petra (in Jordan), the legendary Nabataean capital, was
rediscovered for the West by the Swiss explorer Jean Louis
Burckhardt in 1812. Since then, its remote situation and curiously
carved rock tombs have fascinated westerners. Several artists
during the nineteenth century, including David Roberts, William
Bartlett and Edward Lear, made the difficult and often dangerous
journey to the ancient city.

Edward Lear (1812-1888)

Ruins at Petra   1858

Pen and brown ink over pencil, and watercolour heightened with white
36.4 x 54.4 cm.
Inscribed and dated *Petra 13 Apl.1858*, and numbered *41*; inscribed twice
see Selinuntium and with further notes

Despite insecurity, epilepsy and ill-health, Lear was one of the most intrepid of nineteenth-century artist-travellers. He spent most of his adult life abroad, living for many years in Rome and Corfu, and travelling from there to other parts of Italy, Greece, Albania and the rest of Europe, as well as to the Near East on several occasions. At the age of sixty he toured India and Ceylon.

Of the many dangers and hardships he endured on his travels, Lear's experiences at Petra were especially taxing. The day after he arrived there, on 13 April 1858, the local tribesmen who had gathered around his party demanded payment, and when they threatened violence he was forced to make a quick getaway, though not before he was robbed of 'everything from all my pockets, from dollars and penknives to handkerchiefs and hard-boiled eggs'.

Astonishingly, he had already made several sketches, responding in typically individual manner to Petra's extraordinary combination of impressive ruins and dramatic landscape: 'All the cliffs are of a wonderful colour – like *ham* in stripes; & parts are salmon colour', he wrote to his sister Ann. He made drawings from various viewpoints, including the one exhibited here from 'one of the higher terraces where a mass of fallen columns lies in profuse confusion, not unlike the ruins of the Sicilian Selinunti'. The figure beside the broken columns may well be Feragh ('that jewel among swine'), the black slave lent to Lear for the visit by a local shaykh.

Quotations from: 'A Leaf from the Journals of a Landscape Painter' in H.van Thal, ed., *Edward Lear's Journals: A Selection*, 1952; and Letters to Ann: see Royal Academy of Arts, London, *Edward Lear 1812-1888*, exhibition catalogue by V.Noakes, 1985 (cat.no.25a).

Frederick Charles Cooper (1821-post 1868)

Raft Conveying Winged Bull to Baghdad
Probably c.1850

Watercolour over pencil, with scratching out, on stiff paper
23 x 33 cm.
Lettered with title on former mount

Cooper was an artist from Nottingham who painted in oils and watercolours. In 1849 he was selected by the Trustees of the British Museum to accompany the archaeologist (later diplomat and politician) Austen Henry Layard (see p.49) on his second expedition to excavate the ancient Assyrian cities of Mesopotamia. The Searight Collection contains a large group of drawings by Cooper from this expedition, some showing the remains at Nineveh and Nimrud, and others depicting people and places seen on journeys to the Khabur river (in north-east Syria) and to Kurdistan.

This watercolour depicts one of the massive stone bulls from Nimrud, trussed up and loaded on to its raft, on 22 April 1847, at the beginning of its long journey down the Tigris to Basrah, and thence by ship to England and its new home in the British Museum. The eventful story of its removal from Nimrud and transportation to the raft, kept afloat by 600 inflated goat and sheep-skins, is told by Layard in his account of his first expedition, *Nineveh and its Remains* (1849). Cooper was not present at the time, and probably reconstructed the scene, more as a souvenir of the numerous participants in the event, in the spirit of a team photo, than as an accurate historical record.

Sir Austen Henry Layard GCB (1817-1894)

Reconstruction of the Throne-Room in Ashurnasipal's Palace at Nimrud   Probably 1849

Pen and ink and watercolour, with touches of white
55.5 x 87.8 cm.
Inscribed on the back *Assyrian Court as restored*

Although some details are inaccurate, the scene as a whole is a convincing reconstruction of the lavishly decorated principal ceremonial room in the palace of Ashurnasipal II, King of Assyria in the ninth century BC. The watercolour was reproduced as a lithograph in Layard's *The Monuments of Nineveh* (first series, 1849; Plate 2).

Layard excavated some of the ancient Assyrian cities of Mesopotamia on two expeditions, in 1845-47 and in 1849-51. He made some startling discoveries, including the palaces of Ashurnasipal II at Nimrud, and of Sennacherib in the mound of Kuyunjik at Nineveh.

Layard also pursued a career as a politician and diplomat, serving as British Ambassador in Constantinople, 1877-80. He devoted his later years to the study of art, especially the early Italian Renaissance.

M. Cornelius Le Bruyn (1652-1726/7)

Sculpted relief from Persepolis   c. 1710

Engraving
29.4 x 17.2 cm.
Lettered FIGURE DE L'ESCALIER and numbered 142
Plate 142 from Vol. 2 of Le Bruyn, Travels into Muscovy, Persia
and part of the East-Indies, English edition, London, 1737.

'The principal piece which I endeavoured to procure, was a figure
cut on a stone detached from the rock that formed the grand
staircase. As this stone was thick, I flattered myself that I should
be able to separate the whole figure from it, by dint of time and
patience; but it slivered into three pieces, in spite of all my
precautions.'

Like all early travellers, Le Bruyn had no qualms about removing
pieces of antique sculpture from their sites. He visited Persepolis
in 1704 during a long journey in the East, publishing his account,
first in French in 1711, and later in English. Both this, and an earlier
volume, A Voyage to the Levant (published in his native Dutch, and
also in French and English, 1698-1704), were illustrated with
numerous engravings, and they provided Europeans with the most
detailed picture of the Near East available at the time.

Landscape

LANDSCAPE

Although an artist's primary interest might be the antiquities, the architecture or the people of the Near East, he seldom failed to respond to the natural beauty of its landscape. He might focus on a building – a monastery, a castle or a shaykh's tomb (pp. 62, 52, 57 and 58) – or he might take a wider view of a village or harbour (pp. 54, 55, 64); but it was the landscape, whether of desert, coast, river or mountain, that gave his picture its particular character.

William Daniell RA (1769-1837)

View of the Forts of Marani and Jalali at the Entrance to Muscat Harbour   1793

Watercolour over pencil, on laid paper watermarked *J[?] TAYLOR*
[partly cut away]
22.3 x 30.8 cm.
Inscribed and dated on the original mount *East View of the Forts Jellali & Merani, Muscat   1793* and signed with initials *WD* in the margin

William had accompanied his uncle Thomas Daniell on an extensive tour of India between 1786 and 1793, assisting him with the watercolours that were later published as *Oriental Scenery* (6 parts, 1795-1808). In 1793 the Daniells, intending to return to England, sailed from Bombay to Muscat. Here they heard news of the war between France and England and returned to Bombay, eventually to complete their journey the following year entirely by sea.

Both artists made sketches of the picturesque harbour of Muscat, dominated by the two sixteenth-century fortresses built by the Portugese. Among the oils and watercolours of it that they exhibited at the Royal Academy was William's version of this view, hung in 1831, nearly forty years after their visit. Apart from the Daniells, few European artists visited Muscat, and representations of it are therefore rare.

after Henry Salt FRS FLS (1780-1827)

Muccula in Abyssinia   1809

Coloured aquatint, by Daniel Havell (active 1800-1830),
with additional colouring by hand
53 x 75 cm.
Lettered with title in capitals, and *Drawn by Henry Salt. Engraved by D.
Havell.* and numbered *No. XVIII* and *Published as the Act directs, by William
Miller, Albermarle Street   May 1. 1809.*

'... we came in sight of Muccullah [probably Mekele], in the vicinity
of which, on top of a hill, is a large church, that forms a very
conspicuous object across the plain. The land about the town is in
a high state of cultivation; the soil consists of a rich black loam'.
Henry Salt's description of this and other places he visited in
Abyssinia forms part of George Annesley, Viscount Valentia's
narrative, *Voyages And Travels To India, Ceylon, The Red Sea,
Abyssinia, And Egypt...* (3 vols, 1809). Salt had accompanied

Valentia, as his secretary and draughtsman, on a government
mission to these countries in 1802-06. In addition to the illustrations
for Valentia's volumes, Salt also published a series of aquatints,
*Twenty-four Views taken in St.Helena, the Cape, India, Ceylon,
the Red Sea, Abyssinia and Egypt* (2 vols, 1809), of which this is
Plate XVIII.

Salt returned to Abyssinia in 1809-10 on another government
mission, and published *A Voyage To Abyssinia* in 1814. He then
became British Consul-General in Egypt and, during his term of
office, 1816-27, financed the excavations of G-B.Belzoni, and
formed three large collections of antiquities (see p.32).

Captain Robert Moresby (active 1829-1852)

View of the Town and Harbour of Qusayr on the Red Sea 1829-34

Ink and watercolour
26.2 x 39.2 cm.
Inscribed on the back *Town & Harbor of Cosire Red Sea some Passengers land here from the steamers who wish to visit Thebes* and *No.17* and on a label formerly attached to the back *"Town and Anchorage of Cosire on the Coast of Egypt. here passengers from the Indian Steamers land who wish to visit Thebes" Red Sea by Captn. Robert Moresby the Hon'ble E.I.Co'y's Navy circa 1830*

The development of the steamship in the early nineteenth century meant that the Red Sea became navigable at all seasons, and made possible the establishment of the so-called Overland Route between England and India, via Egypt. Marine surveys were carried out to determine the best routes and the most convenient coaling stations for steamers along the coasts of the Red Sea, and the Gulfs of Suez and Aqaba. Moresby was Commander of the East India Company's ship *Palinurus*, which took part in one of these surveys between 1829 and 1834. Their findings were published by the East India Company in *Sailing Directions for the Red Sea* (1841), where Qusayr is described as containing about 2,000 inhabitants. Here travellers, instead of sailing on up to Suez, could disembark and continue their journey overland across the desert to the Nile and thence to Cairo.

Seven other watercolours done by Moresby during this survey are in the Searight Collection (with five more at the National Maritime Museum, Greenwich). Though probably trained as a draughtsman at a naval academy, his compositions pay little regard to pictorial convention and are refreshingly idiosyncratic.

William Purser (c.1790-c.1852)

Meadow of the Sweet Waters of Asia,
Constantinople   1820s-30s

Watercolour and bodycolour, heightened with white, over pencil,
on thick paper
30.3 x 45.1 cm.
Signed *W. Purser.*

The 'Sweet Waters of Asia' was the name given by Europeans in
late Ottoman times to two streams, the Göksu and the Küçüksu,
which flowed into the Bosphorus near the Anadolu Hisarı (Castle
of Asia). The meadow in between became a favourite resort for the
fashionable élite of Ottoman and European society. Here came the
women and children in their brightly painted *arabas* (ox-drawn
carriages) and the men on horseback, to picnic, smoke, chat,
wander, and while away the hours in a peaceful environment,
away from the turmoil of the city. It was a picturesque scene that
few European artists could resist, the natural beauty of the
landscape offset by the artifice of the little late baroque fountain of
Mihrişah Sultan, mother of Selim III, on the shore.

This is one of four similarly picturesque views by Purser of
Constantinople and its environs, in the Searight Collection. Purser
was probably there sometime during the 1820s and/or 1830s, but
under what circumstances is not recorded.

Thomas Allom FRIBA (1804-1872)

Summer Houses and the Castle of Europe, on the Bosphorus   1846

Watercolour, heightened with white, over pencil
19.4 x 30.7 cm.
Signed and dated *T. Allom.   1846*; inscribed on the back *The Bosphorus, with the Castles of Europe & Asia   1846.*

The shores of the Bosphorus attracted the attention of many artists. A favourite subject was the romantic medieval fortress, Rumeli Hisarı, which dominates the narrowest part of the straits, opposite its companion on the Asian shore, Anadolu Hisarı, seen in the distance in Allom's view. Allom has made a picturesque juxtaposition of the stone crenellations of the castle with the fretted wooden balconies of the houses, or *yalıs*, that 150 years ago were a distinctive feature of the villages along the Bosphorus.

Although he trained and practised as an architect, Allom is better known as a topographical artist. Like Bartlett (p.46) he travelled widely and contributed illustrations to numerous books on places in Europe, the Near East and even China, published during the 1830s and 1840s. Few details of his journeys are known but he appears to have visited Turkey and Palestine in about 1838. (See also p.117.)

Jules-Joseph-Augustin Laurens (1825-1901)

Route de Casbinn à Tèhèran Effet de neige   1848

Pencil, on thin paper
25.2 x 42.5 cm.
Signed *Jules Laurens*; inscribed with title and dated *1848*

In 1846, only a few years after Flandin and Coste (see pp.77 & 84) had accompanied an official French mission to Persia, another governmental expedition, led by the geographer Xavier Hommaire de Hell, was sent to carry out further investigations. This time Laurens, a young artist who had studied in the *atelier* of Paul Delaroche, was employed to record the course of their journey in a series of images that, after his return in 1849, were used to illustrate Hommmaire de Hell's *Voyage en Turquie et en Perse* (4 vols and atlas, 1854-60). Despite the rigours of the journey and an attack of fever, Laurens filled several sketch-books with his drawings of the people and landscapes they encountered. This one was made in February 1848, as they neared Tehran on the road from Qazvin, in temperatures well below zero (−24° was recorded one day). Despite the physical discomfort, Laurens's sensitive draughtsmanship is well illustrated in the carefully observed detail and gentle rhythms of this composition.

Adrien Dauzats (1804-1868)

Les Portes de Fer   1846

Watercolour, touched with bodycolour
24.3 x 32.1 cm.
Inscribed, signed and dated *Bibans A.Dauzats. 1846,* and on the former
mount *Les Portes de Fer   A:Dauzats   No.11.*

On 28 October 1839 Dauzats accompanied a division of the French
army, consisting of 3,000 men, through the smaller of the two
gorges, known as the Portes de Fer (Gates of Iron), which cut
through the Jurjura mountains in Kabylia, Algeria. Their journey
from Sétif to Algiers was part of a wider French operation, led by
the duc d'Orleans, to establish political and military hegemony
in Algeria.

Dauzats's composition makes full use of the dramatic potential of
the scenery. The dark rock walls of the defile fill the picture space
almost entirely, towering over the tiny figures of the soldiers, and
creating a feeling of claustrophobia. The favourite romantic theme
of the insignificance of man in the face of the mighty forces of nature
is a recurrent one in Dauzats's work. He painted several views of
the Portes de Fer in both oil and watercolour, including five that
were reproduced for the *Journal de l'Expédition des Portes de Fer*
(1841), compiled by the poet Charles Nodier. Powerful and
atmospheric compositions such as these have established a
significant place for Dauzats in the history of French Orientalism.

Carlo Bossoli (1815-1884)

Sebastopol, as seen from the Northern Forts
1856

Lithograph, with three tint-stones, by Day & Son, coloured by hand
25.5 x 38.8 cm
Inscribed *Sebastopol from the Northern Forts*

This is Plate 7 from *The Beautiful Scenery And Chief Places Of Interest Throughout The Crimea From Paintings By Carlo Bossoli*, published by Day & Son in 1856. The view is described in the publication: 'In front are the whole of the Town and the Military Port; on the right, Fort St.Nicholas and Fort Alexander; and on the left, the great harbour of Inkerman Bay.' Also included, to add local colour, are some ships at anchor and, in the foreground, several women bathers.

The war in the Crimea during 1854-56 aroused considerable interest in Britain, not just in the fortunes of the battles, but also in the scenery of the whole region. Bossoli's lavish publication, with fifty-two colour plates, showing Sebastopol, Balaklava, Inkerman, Kertch and other places made famous by the hostilities, was designed to meet popular demand for information about the Crimea. Bossoli, though born in Lugano, had grown up in Odessa, where his precocious artistic abilities had been encouraged by Countess Vorontsov, wife of the wealthy and powerful governor of southern Russia. He had returned to Europe with his family in the mid-1840s and, on the outbreak of the Crimean War, ten years later, travelled to London, where his landscapes met with great success.

Maria Harriett Mathias, née Rawstorne
(active 1850s)

Crusader's Castle on the Island of Graia, Gulf of Aqaba   1857

Watercolour over pencil
25.3 x 35.9 cm.
Inscribed and dated *Crusaders Castle   Graia Gulph of Akabah   May 11. 1857*

Gazirat Faraun, an island near the head of the Gulf of Aqaba, is viewed from Sinai, on the western shore, looking across to Arabia. The castle, hardly distinguishable from its rocky environment, was built by Baldwin I of Jerusalem in about 1115. This delightful watercolour, and nine others in the Searight Collection, were originally part of an album of views made by Mrs Mathias during her tour of Egypt and the Levant with her husband and brother-in-law in 1856-57. Sketch-book in one hand and Murray's guide-book in the other, she was typical of the non-specialist but interested and informed tourists who were then travelling in increasing numbers to the area. The album is evidence that she was a competent amateur watercolourist, but very little else is known about her.

Richard Beavis RWS (1824-1896)

Monastery of Saint Catherine, Sinai   1875

Pencil, charcoal and watercolour, heightened with white, on stiff paper
35.4 x 52.7 cm.
Signed with initials *RB*, inscribed *The Convent, Mount Sinai   South East
view* and dated, partly illegibly, [... *25/75*]

The fine pencil lines, delicate shading and pale tonalities of this
watercolour admirably convey the bright sunlight of the region and
the stark mountainous terrain in which the monastery is situated.
Beavis visited it in 1875, as he passed through Sinai on his way from
Egypt to Palestine. Travellers on this journey usually stopped at
the monastery, founded in the fourth century AD as a sanctuary
around the site of the Burning Bush (*Exodus:* 3).

As well as the drawings and watercolours made on and
immediately after this trip, Beavis exhibited a few Orientalist
paintings during the late 1870s, but is better known for his
landscapes, atmospheric coastal views, and scenes of rustic life.

Henry Lamb RA (1885-1959)

Palestine Landscape   1917-18

Watercolour over pencil, with additional pencil lines
17.4 x 24.8 cm.

Lamb was one of a group of young artists pioneering new ways of
representing landscape in the years immediately before the First
World War. He exhibited at the New England Art Club and was a
member of the Camden Town and London Groups of artists.
During the War he served as Official War Artist in Macedonia,
Palestine and France, and presumably did this watercolour while
in Palestine in 1917-18. His landscape includes no readily
identifiable features, for his interests lay in expressing its mood
through colour and form rather than in delineating its
topographical elements.

Charles William Cain (1893-1962)

Al Kifil on the Euphrates, Mesopotamia   c.1927

Drypoint
38 x 55.5 cm.
Signed with monogram *CWC* and in ink *Charles W. Cain;* inscribed in pencil
in another hand *Kifl, River Euphrates, Mesopotamia.* and *Exhibited in Royal
Scottish Academy 1927 & Paris 1927*

During the First World War, Cain was sent to India and
Mesopotamia as a War Artist. Afterwards he established his
reputation in London and Paris with etchings and paintings based
on material drawn from these countries. Sixteen etchings of
Mesopotamia in the Searight Collection show his interest in several
different aspects of the country (now Iraq), including life in the
villages on the banks of the Euphrates, the various river craft, the
houses, mosques and shaykh's tombs, and the women performing
their daily tasks.

In the example shown here he makes subtle use of the drypoint
technique to achieve striking effects, notably the reflections on the
river's surface, and the dramatic contrast of dazzling light and
dense shadow on the buildings.

Cities

CITIES

The cities of the Near East most frequented by western travellers were Cairo, Jerusalem and Constantinople (Istanbul). For many, these great metropolises, with their famous mosques, their noisy bazaars and their colourfully dressed people, epitomised the Orient.

David Roberts spent over a month in Cairo, in 1838-39, drawing the streets and mosques. 'Now that I am again in Cairo I am delighted with it', he wrote in his Journal, '. . . some of the mosques are of the most extraordinary description, of which there are not less than 400'. A few years later William Thackeray was also entranced: 'I never saw such a variety of architecture, of life, of picturesqueness, of brilliant colour, and light and shade. There is a picture in every street, and at every bazaar stall.' (*Notes of a Journey from Cornhill to Grand Cairo*, 1846).

Constantinople, too, inspired wonder and amazement. Murray's *Handbook for Travellers in Turkey* quoted a western visitor's typical response: 'At last, Constantinople rose in all its grandeur before us. With eyes riveted on the expanding splendours, I watched, as they rose out of the bosom of the surrounding waters, the pointed minarets – the swelling cupolas – and the innumerable habitations, either stretching along the jagged shore, or reflecting their image in the mirror of the deep, or creeping up the crested mountain, and tracing their outline in the expanse of the sky.' Such effusions were not for Alexander Kinglake who commented in *Eothen* with his usual pithy humour: 'Even if we don't take part in the chant about "mosques and minarets" we can still yield praises to Stamboul.'

Frans Hogenberg (before 1540-c. 1592)

Alexandria c.1575

Plate 56 from Georg Braun & Frans Hogenberg, *Civitates Orbis Terrarum, De praecipuis totius universi urbibus. liber secundus*
Etching, coloured by hand
36.1 x 47.7 cm.
Lettered in Latin with title and key and with brief historical description; on the back of the sheet numbered *56* and lettered with long Latin text

Civitates Orbis Terrarum was conceived as an atlas of city plans and views to accompany Ortelius's atlas *Theatrum Orbis Terrarum* (1570). It eventually comprised six books published 1572-1618, in many editions, mostly in Cologne. Many of the plates were after drawings by the topographical artist Joris (or Georg) Hoefnagel (1542-1600), but the example here appears to have been based on an unidentified Italian engraving, redrawn and engraved for this publication by Hogenberg. The representation of the city is more fanciful than factual. Taken from the traditional bird's eye view, in order to include significant features and monuments (notably Pompey's Column and Cleopatra's Needles), it is set in a picturesque landscape in which figures of the inhabitants (and, in this case, camels) are variously placed to add local flavour; here numerous ships have taken the place of the usual foreground figures, to emphasise Alexandria's maritime importance.

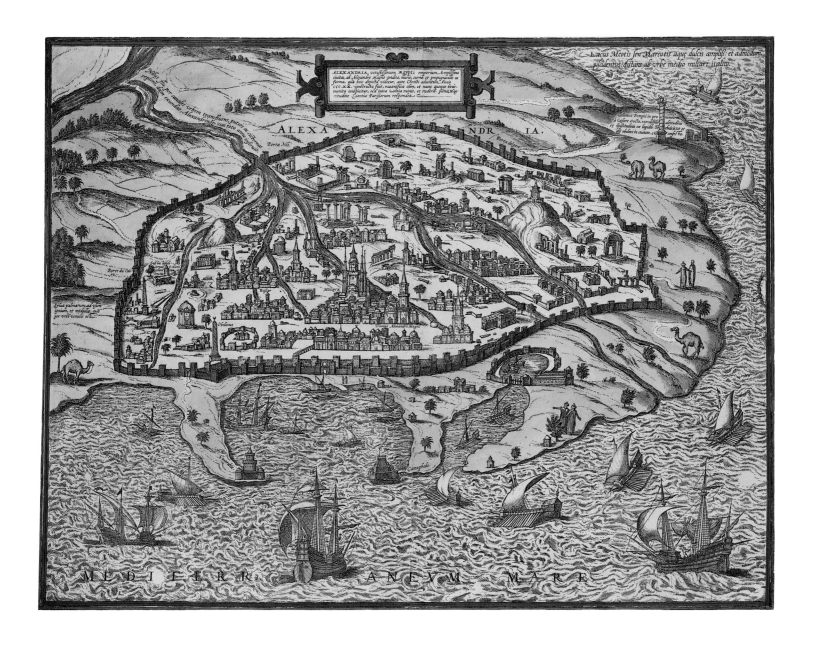

ALEXANDRIA

MEDITERRANEUM MARE

67

David Roberts RA (1796-1864)

Grand Cairo   1839-49

Watercolour and bodycolour over pencil
31.8 x 48 cm.
Inscribed with title and dated *Jany 27th 1839.* and, very faintly,
Gate of Citizenib [...]

This view was reproduced as a lithograph by Louis Haghe in Roberts's *Egypt & Nubia* (1846-49; Vol.III) with the incorrect title, *Cairo from the Gate of Citizenib, looking towards the Desert of Suez*. The viewpoint is not in fact from Citizenib (modern Sayidah Zaynab) as Roberts thought, but from Tel Zaynum to the south of Cairo. The main monuments in the foreground are, from left to right, the tombs of Fatimah Khatun and of Sultan Khalil (still extant), an unidentified and now destroyed mosque or tomb, and, on the far right, the mosque of Sayidah Nafisah (since rebuilt). In the right background is the Citadel and on the left the Madrasah of Sultan Hassan. The high viewpoint, looking down on the varied contours of the domes and minarets of the city, and the delicate pink glow with which they are suffused, make this one of Roberts's most striking Eastern watercolours.

Roberts's images of the Near East are widely known now, as in his own time, through the series of lithographs published between 1842 and 1849 as *The Holy Land, Syria, Idumea, Arabia, Egypt & Nubia*. Each of the 247 lithographs was after a watercolour by Roberts that was worked up from sketches made during his tour of the Near East in 1838-39. He was among the earliest of many professional and independent European artists to visit the area in search of new and exotic pictorial material and when he left he knew that he carried 'one of the richest folios that ever left the East'. This claim was justified by the huge success not only of his publication but also of the numerous oils with oriental subjects that he painted as a result of his trip.

Henry Warren PNWS KL (1794-1879)

View of the Haram al-Sharif with the Dome of the Rock, Jerusalem   Probably 1861-62

Watercolour and bodycolour, heightened with white, over pencil
20.9 x 36.6 cm.
Signed *H. Warren.*

The Haram al-Sharif is a focal point for two great religions: it is the site of the Jewish Temple, first built by Solomon, and is also the second most important place of pilgrimage for Muslims (see p.80). As an Old Testament site it is also of interest to Christians, and Warren's view, with the Dome of the Rock in the centre, was engraved for the Revd John Fleetwood's *The Life of Our Lord and Saviour Jesus Christ* (1854). The watercolour was based on a sketch by the sculptor and draughtsman, Joseph Bonomi (1796-1878), who had visited Jerusalem in 1833. Warren himself apparently never went to Jerusalem, or indeed anywhere in the Near East, despite the preponderance of oriental subjects in his work. He painted many large and elaborate watercolours, often with literary or biblical themes, which, when exhibited at the New Society of Painters in Water-Colours, were acclaimed for their skill and authenticity. He was President of the NWS 1839-73, and was awarded the Belgian honour of Knight of the Order of Leopold.

Amadeo, Fifth Count Preziosi (1816-1882)

The Entrance to the Golden Horn, Constantinople
1853

Watercolour over pencil, with scratching out and touches of white
51.5 x 72.5 cm.
Inscribed, signed and dated *Constantinople by Preziosi 1853*

The entrance to the Golden Horn was one of the finest natural harbours in the world. In it Preziosi shows examples of the type of craft then plying the waters of the Bosphorus: on the left a light *kayık* used to ferry passengers short distances between the Asiatic and the European shores, but easily overturned in rough weather; the heavy barge in the centre could transport people to and from the villages further up the Bosphorus; behind this at anchor is a trading galley. The oarsmen or *kayıkcilar* row with the strange local form of oar with bulbous handles. In the background some of the principal features of the city can be made out, including on the left Saray Burnu (Seraglio Point), with the gardens and pavilions of Topkapı spreading up the hillside, and on the right Pera and Galata (Beyoğlu) with the Galata fire-tower on the skyline and the buildings of Tophane on the shore.

Preziosi was of noble Maltese birth, but against the wishes of his family rejected their chosen profession of the law to become an artist. From 1842 until his death forty years later, he lived and worked in Constantinople, renowned for his vibrant and evocative images of the cosmopolitan peoples and interesting places of the city. He also became known in western Europe because many travellers (including in 1869 the Prince of Wales) took his pictures home as souvenirs of their visit. Demand for his work prompted the publication in Paris in 1858 of a series of lithographs, *Stamboul Recollections of Eastern Life*. (See also p.135.)

William Lionel Wyllie RA RI (1851-1931)

The Golden Horn, Constantinople   c.1910

Drypoint
20.3 x 25.5 cm.
Signed in pencil *WL Wyllie*

Wyllie's marine paintings and etchings were much admired during
his lifetime, and, after a period of neglect, they are now again
popular. He portrayed all manner of sailing and steam craft and is
particularly renowned for his atmospheric views of the Thames
and Medway. This view of the Golden Horn at Constantinople is
an unusual subject for Wyllie, but it is no less evocative. The
harbour is as full of shipping as Preziosi's view of thirty years earlier
(p.70), and, although it contains less of a panoramic sweep of the
city, its locality is just as firmly pinpointed by the dominance on
the skyline of the two mosques, the Süleymaniye on the left and
the Fatih Camii on the right.

Giuseppe Schranz (1803-after 1853)

Constantinople and the Bosphorus from Scutari
c.1835

Pencil
35.5 x 71.3 cm.

This view is from the shore at Üsküdar (formerly Scutari) and looks across the Bosphorus towards the mouth of the Golden Horn, with Saray Burnu (Seraglio Point) on the left and Kız Kulesi (or Leander's Tower) on the extreme right.

Like his brother Antonio (p.40), Giuseppe Schranz was a topographical artist; his speciality was panoramic views of Constantinople and the Bosphorus. He appears to have been based there from the mid-1830s, returning to Malta only temporarily. Demand for his work was especially high during the early and mid-1850s as a result of the interest in the area generated by hostilities in the Crimea, and several of his panoramic views were published as lithographs.

ARCHITECTURE
Religious and Secular

During the nineteenth century Muslim attitudes to the presence of foreigners in their sacred buildings changed dramatically. In 1833 Frederick Catherwood (see p.31) succeeded in making the first complete survey of the Dome of the Rock in Jerusalem, but only a mixture of luck and bravado had saved him from the fury of the mob, indignant at his profanation of their shrine. By the 1860s, however, neither Rear-Admiral Paris nor Carl Werner (see p.80) appeared to experience much difficulty in gaining access to and sketching inside the Dome. Likewise in Cairo, in 1838-39, David Roberts (see p.68) was granted permission to sketch inside the mosques, provided he wore Turkish dress, shaved off his whiskers and did not use hog's-hair brushes. Even so, and despite the protection of a guide, he was subjected to some harassment. But in the 1880s, in Tlemçen, Fabrizi (or a contemporary – see p.82) appears to have been allowed to represent Muslims at prayer in one of the holiest shrines in North Africa.

Although the portrayal of secular architecture did not present the same problems as religious architecture, it was less often the object of artists' attention. Frank Dillon (pp.85-87) was one of the few artists not also an architect, to depict interior as well as exterior views of several domestic Islamic buildings.

William Page (1794-1872)

Fountain of Tophana, Constantinople   1829

Etching and aquatint, by R.G.Reeve (active c.1811-c.1837),
printed in brown and green, with additional colouring by hand
Trimmed to 60.6 x 82.3 cm.
Lettered with title and *W. Page, Delint.   R.G. Reeve, Sculpt.*

The original watercolour for this print was exhibited at the Royal Academy in 1825 with a companion, *Fountain of Babhoumayoun or Sublime Porte*, probably identifiable with a watercolour in the Searight Collection. Both are unusually large and impressive examples of Page's work. The focus of each composition is an elaborately decorated early eighteenth-century street-fountain, both magnificent examples of Ottoman baroque architecture. The dome and widely-overhanging eaves of the Tophane Çeşmeşi were later damaged and, although the building has recently been restored, Page's aquatint shows it in its original splendour. The fountain, beside the Kılıç Ali Paşa Camii, was the centre of life in the locality. The busy street market seen here includes traders selling clothes and other textiles, fruit and vegetables, and refreshments such as *mahallebi* (milk-puddings).

Page first visited Greece and Turkey 1816-24, and may also have travelled there later in the 1820s and in the 1830s. These trips provided material for numerous picturesque scenes of local people (see p.125) and buildings, of which there are several in the Searight Collection.

Prosper Georges Antoine Marilhat (1811-1847)

The Darb al-Ahmar, Cairo   1831-32

Pencil and red chalk
47.4 x 32.5 cm.

This masterly drawing represents a view looking north along part of the Darb al-Ahmar (now Sharia Bab al-Wazir). On the right is a corner of the Palace of Alin Aq (now almost destroyed); next, the Mosque and Tomb of Amir Khayrbak; behind this, the Mosque of Aqsunqur, also known as the Blue Mosque or the Mosque of Ibrahim Agha. It is an excellent example of Marilhat's sensitive use of his chosen media – pencil and red chalk – not only to render precisely each architectural detail but also to convey the contrasts of light and shade, and to suggest the hot, dusty atmosphere of the Cairo street.

Marilhat travelled in the Near East with the botanist and traveller Baron Karl von Hügel in 1831-32, and stayed on in Egypt for a further year making topographical studies, such as the one shown here, as well as portraits of notable people, including Muhammad Ali, Viceroy of Egypt. After his return to France he exhibited Orientalist paintings for ten years. These won great critical acclaim, and many engravings and lithographs after his work were published. Sadly, he developed a debilitating mental illness and died insane.

This, and the view by Flandin (p.77), show exteriors of Islamic buildings in two cities renowned for the quality of their Islamic architecture – Cairo and Isfahan.

Eugène-Napoléon Flandin (1809-1876)

The Meidan-i-Shah, Isfahan   1841

Watercolour over pencil
21.5 x 34.6 cm.
Signed, inscribed and dated *Eug. Flandin. Ispahan. 1841.*; inscribed on the
back *l'hippodrome à Ispahan* and on the mount, in a different hand,
Atmeidan Schah Ispahan

The *maydan* was created as a polo-ground by Shah Abbas soon after
he moved his capital to Isfahan in the early seventeenth century.
Around it were erected a series of splendid buildings. On the far
side is the Masjid-i-Shah (1612-37), built at an angle to the entrance
portal in order to achieve the correct orientation towards Mecca; on
the right, Ali Qapu, the gatehouse of the palace complex, with its
enormous wooden loggia projecting over the square from which
the royal family could view the ceremonies and sporting events
taking place below.

Flandin was in Isfahan in 1840 and 1841 while taking part in a
French diplomatic mission led by Edouard de Sercey to the Shah
of Persia. He and fellow artist Pascal Coste (see p.84) were
employed to record Persia's ancient and Islamic monuments, and
after their return to France they published jointly eight volumes of
text and plates entitled *Voyage en Perse* [1843-54]. A version of the
watercolour shown here is Plate LIV in the *Perse Moderne* volume
of the publication.

Flandin also travelled elsewhere in the Near East, accompanying
the French military campaign in Algeria in 1837 and an
archaeological expedition to Khorsabad in Mesopotamia in 1844.
Several volumes of his drawings from these travels are in the
Victoria and Albert Museum. They served as material not only
for illustrated publications but also for oil and watercolour
paintings exhibited at the Salon in Paris, including a view of the
Masjid-i-Shah.

John Frederick Lewis RA POWCS (1805-1875)

Interior of Haghia Sophia, Constantinople 1840/41

Pencil, chalk and watercolour, heightened with white
36.2 x 47.6 cm.

Lewis is famous for the exquisite paintings of oriental life that he exhibited in London in the mid-nineteenth century. Though lesser known, the watercolour sketches he made while living in Turkey and Egypt are also exceptional. In the example shown here, the vast interior space of Haghia Sophia is conveyed with an apparent minimum of effort. The delicately rendered pencil framework is given substance by a judicious use of white highlights and sparingly applied touches of colour, notably in the tiny pinpoints of red for the fezzes of members of the congregation. The view is of the eastern end of the basilica, at that time used as a mosque, with the *minbar* (pulpit) to the right and the *müezzin mahfili* (dais for the *müezzin*) to the left. On the piers hang square *levhas* (painted wooden plaques), bearing the Sacred Islamic Names, which, during the restorations carried out by the Fossati brothers later in the 1840s, were replaced by round ones.

Lewis spent about a year in Constantinople from October 1840 before continuing on to Egypt (p.131), where he lived for nearly a decade, returning to England in 1851.

after Gaspard Fossati (1809-1883)
and Alexius Gayer (1816-1883)

Façade Principale De Ste.Sophie, Prise De La Cour
Du Médressé   1852

Lithograph, with two tint stones, by Louis Haghe (1806-1885),
coloured by hand
Cut to 27.2 x 37.4 cm.
Numbered twice *Planche 16* and lettered *Gayer del. Fossati dirext, – L.Haghe,*
lith.   London. Published June 1st.1852, by P & D.Colnaghi & Co. 13 & 14,
Pall Mall East.   Day & Son. Lithrs. to the Queen.

Built by the Emperor Justinian in AD 532-37, Haghia Sophia is a
monument to the Golden Age of the Byzantine Empire. After the
fall of Constantinople to the Turks in 1453, Sultan Mehmet II, the
Conqueror, ordered it to be converted into a mosque.

This is a plate from the deluxe edition of Fossati's *Aya Sofia*
Constantinople, published by P & D.Colnaghi in 1852. The
publication commemorated the restoration work carried out on
parts of Haghia Sophia during 1847-49 by Gaspard and his brother
Giuseppe, on a commission from Sultan Abdul Mecit I. The Fossati
brothers were Swiss architects who studied in Italy; they spent
several years in Constantinople, working on various religious
buildings in the city. Gayer, a German artist, was also in
Constantinople at the time.

79

after Rear-Admiral François Edmond Paris

Chapelle du Saint Sépulcre [Jerusalem] 1862

Colour lithograph, by Hubert Clerget (1818-1899) and Jules Gaildreau
(1816-1898)
49.2 x 35.4 cm. (arched top)
Lettered with title of album and plate in capitals, and *Paris del. H.Clerget
lith. Fig. par Gaildreau. Arthus Bertrand Editeur. Imp Lemercier r.de Seine
57 Paris*
Plate 3 from Paris, *Souvenirs de Jérusalem,* Paris, 1862.

Rear-admiral Paris appears to have been attached to the French
fleet in the Mediterranean in about 1860, and to have been among
those given the opportunity of visiting Jerusalem. The drawings
that he made there were lithographed for this album. The plate
illustrated here is one of several that shows groups of fellow officers
and sailors sightseeing. In 1869 he was among the many European
dignitaries who attended the opening of the Suez Canal (see p.96).

Carl Friedrich Heinrich Werner (1808-1894)

Interior of the Dome of the Rock, Jerusalem 1863

Watercolour
50.3 x 34.7 cm.
Signed and dated *C. Werner. f. 1863*

Although German by birth, Werner lived for nearly twenty years
in Rome, and also frequently visited and exhibited in London. He
visited Palestine and Egypt in 1862-64. His highly polished
watercolour technique conveys well the opulence and suffused
light of the interior of the Dome of the Rock. Here he shows the
inner of the two ambulatories with its pillars and columns of
different coloured marbles, its gilded capitals and its *ablaq* (pied)
stonework. Built by the Ummayyad Caliph, Abd al-Malik, in
AD 687-91, the shrine surrounds the rock from which Muhammad
ascended to Heaven on his horse, Buraq, and is one of Islam's most
sacred buildings. The rock is also revered in Jewish tradition as the
site where Abraham offered Isaac as a sacrifice.

The watercolour was reproduced as a colour lithograph (also in the
Searight Collection) with the erroneous title, *Interior of the Mosque
of Omar,* in C. Werner's *Jerusalem, Bethlehem and the Holy Places*
(1865-66).

S.Fabrizi (active 1880s)

Mosque of Sidi Bu Madyan, Tlemçen   1881

Watercolour, with gum, over pencil on stiff paper
56.5 x 38.5 cm.
Signed, inscribed and dated *S.Fabrizi Tlemcen. 1881.*

Fabrizi's skill as a draughtsman and colourist is evident in this watercolour, but very little is known about him. His style and subject matter were clearly similar to those of a group of Italian Orientalist artists working in Rome in the 1870s and 1880s, notably Enrico Tarengi, Gustavo Simoni and Filippo Bartolini. All these artists painted numerous scenes of life in North Africa – in the mosques, the streets and the desert – although some had never been there and based their compositions on photographs.

The mosque adjoins the shrine of Sidi Bu Madyan, a twelfth-century holy-man, and was built by the Marinid dynasty in 1339. Fabrizi's view shows clearly the richly carved stucco decoration framing the simple horseshoe arches; through one of these is seen the tiled *mihrab* (niche indicating the direction of Mecca) and the wooden *minbar* (pulpit). Fabrizi has captured the moment after the formal prayers when each worshipper makes a personal supplication to Allah, holding his hands out in a gesture to receive His blessing.

Pascal-Xavier Coste (1787-1879)

Vue De La Porte Et Détails Des Boutiques De l'Okél De Qayd-Bey   1818-22

Pencil and watercolour
On 2 sheets; size of page 42.4 x 57.3 cm.
Lettered with title in capitals; signed *P. Coste, Delin.* and inscribed
Okél de Kaid-Bey
Page from a volume, quarter bound in green morocco, titled and incorrectly
dated on the spine *DRAWINGS OF OLD CAIRO BY P.COSTE 1815.*, containing
architectural drawings for Coste, *Architecture Arabe, ou Monuments du Kaire,*
Paris, 1837 & 1839.

Coste's magnificent volume of architectural drawings was the first
to show the Islamic buildings of Cairo in detail. The page shown
here exemplifies the combination of careful observation and
meticulous draughtsmanship that make the volume outstanding.
Coste made the drawings in Cairo between 1818 and 1822 while
working for Muhammad Ali, but did not publish them until 1837
due to protracted negotiations with Robert Hay, who purchased
them from Coste with exclusive rights of publication but then failed
to meet the deadline imposed by the artist. In its wide ranging and

detailed depiction of Cairo's Islamic architectural decoration,
Coste's *Architecture Arabe* was rivalled by few other nineteenth-
century publications.

The Wikalah (hostel) of Sultan Qayt-Bey, built in 1477, is situated
to the south of al-Azhar. Only the façade now remains, and Coste's
drawing is therefore a valuable record of the former elegance of its
stonework, combining carved arabesque panels with *ablaq* (pied)
decoration.

Coste was an architect who executed several commissions in his
native Marseilles, including the Bourse. He also travelled
extensively in Europe, Russia and North Africa, and with fellow
artist Eugène Flandin (see p.77), accompanied a French diplomatic
mission to Persia in 1839-42.

Frank Dillon RI (1823-1909)

Al-Mahkamah (Court of the Cadi), Cairo   1869

Watercolour and bodycolour over pencil, on thick paper
29.7 x 52.7 cm.
Inscribed and dated *El Mahkemeh or Court of the Cadi   Cairo   Decr 5th 1869.*,
and numbered *16*

The *maqad* (loggia) depicted here, with its five slightly pointed
horseshoe arches and *ablaq* (pied) stonework, is all that remains of
the Mamluk palace of Amir Mamay, built in 1496. The area, known
popularly as the Bayt al-Qadi (House of the Judge), was the seat of
a court (*al-mahkamah*) during the Ottoman administration in Egypt.

Dillon exhibited numerous oil paintings and watercolours in
London galleries, including the Royal Academy, over a period of
more than fifty years, but is not so well known today as other
nineteenth-century Orientalist painters. He visited Egypt on four
occasions between 1854 and 1874, and, with the notable exception
of J.F.Lewis (p.78), was almost alone among fellow British artists
in focussing his attention on Cairo's domestic Islamic architecture.

85

William J. Tipping (1816-1897)

Courtyard of a House in Damascus   1840

Pencil, heightened with white
22 x 21.1 cm.
Signed with initials, *WT.*, inscribed and dated *Damas. 15 Mars: 40.*

Tipping was a respected amateur archaeologist who from 1839
spent seven years in the Near East exploring ancient ruins. In
addition to well known sites, such as the Parthenon, he visited
others off the beaten track, like Jarash (now in Jordan) and Masada.
In 1864 he was elected a member of the Society of Antiquaries.

His parallel interest in more modern architecture is displayed
in this drawing of an unidentified Damascus house, with its
hawsh (open courtyard), fountain and *takhtabush* (recessed
area for sitting).

Frank Dillon RI (1823-1909)

Interior of a Room in the House of Shaykh Sadat, Cairo   c.1875

Gouache
75 x 59.5 cm.

This splendid painting represents the *qaah* or principal room in the
women's apartments of the Bayt al-Sadat, a fine house still extant
near the Sharia al-Gammamiz. The room is sumptuously decorated
with a painted and carved wooden ceiling; stained glass windows
and *mashrabiyyah* (lattice-work) shutters; a carved *dulab* (cupboard)
without the usual Chinese or Persian ceramics in the recesses; some
provincial Ottoman tiles from Damascus on the wall; cushions with
multicoloured woollen covers on the divan; and a carpet and a
small table, inlaid with mother-of-pearl, on the floor.

In the 1870s Dillon made a collection of Islamic works of art with
which he created an 'Arab studio' in his house in Kensington. It
was inspired by rooms like the one shown here. Several other
watercolours of Mamluk houses in Cairo are in the Victoria and
Albert Museum, including another view of this room, engraved in
Georg Ebers's *Egypt: Descriptive, Historical, and Picturesque* (Vol.II,
1879), with the title *Ka'ah in the Harem of Sheykh Sadat, Cairo.*

Richard Phené Spiers FRIBA FSA (1838-1916)

The Great Khan, Damascus   1866

Watercolour over pencil
36.4 x 25.8 cm.
Signed *R.Phené Spiers.;* lettered with title and name of artist
on former mount

Spiers was an architect, known better for his teaching and writing
on the subject than as a practitioner. In 1865-66 he toured the Near
East on a travelling studentship from the Royal Academy, studying
antique as well as Islamic architecture. On his return he exhibited
several pictures with Eastern subjects at the Royal Academy, one
of which, *Great Khan at Damascus*, may have been this or a similar
watercolour. The building represented is probably the sixteenth-
century Khan of Asad Pasha al-Azam, now destroyed. With its
massive piers, arches and pendentives raising the domes,
strikingly decorated with *ablaq* (pied) stonework, it was clearly an
impressive building, large enough to house many merchants with
their merchandise.

EAST MEETS WEST
Potentates and dignitaries

Before the eighteenth century, contacts between Europe and the Near East were mostly commercial. English merchants travelled to the Levant from the mid-fifteenth century onwards, and the Levant Company, which held a monopoly on trade in the area, was established in 1581. Its officials initiated diplomatic relations between Britain and the Ottoman Empire and prepared the way for greater political interest in the area in the nineteenth century.

Many of the audiences given by Eastern and Western rulers to foreign ambassadors were recorded by artists; Mather Brown's picture is just one example. Spilsbury's composition (p.92) records an aspect of Britain's early political contacts with Syria and Palestine. During the nineteenth century ordinary individuals were able to travel to the Levant and arrange their own meetings with local potentates; one such occasion was recorded by an amateur artist (p.93). By the end of the century many European countries had a vested interest in the Near East. The histories of the two regions were so inextricably linked that they were a common subject for comment in popular magazines, such as *Punch* (p.97).

after Mather Brown (1761-1831)

His Majesty and the Officers of State Receiving The Turkish Ambassador and Suit. 1797

Stipple, line engraving and etching, by Daniel Orme (c.1766- after 1832) 48.5 x 61 cm.
Lettered with title and dedication to *His Grace The Duke of Leeds Governor of the United Turkey Company* and *Painted by M.Brown Historical Painter to their R.H. The Duke & Duchess of York Engraved by D.Orme Historical Engraver to his Majesty & his R.H. the Prince of Wales.*, and with a key to the principal figures. Also lettered *Sold & Published Jany. 1 1797, by Edwd. Orme Junr. No.25, Conduit Street, Hanover Square.*

A new phase in Anglo-Ottoman relations is here recorded. Until the end of the eighteenth century the Ottoman Empire had had no permanent diplomatic representation in Europe, only a handful of envoys having been sent on isolated special missions. In 1792, as part of his westward looking reforms, Selim III (see p.94) resolved to establish permanent Ottoman embassies in the major European capitals. The first of these was in London, where the Ambassador, Yusuf Ağă Efendi was received at Court in December 1793. It is probably he, along with his retinue, who is being presented to King George III by the Foreign Secretary, Lord Grenville. Also prominent in the King's entourage, on his right, is his Prime Minister, William Pitt the Younger.

Mather Brown was an American painter who arrived in London in 1781 and became a pupil of Benjamin West. His portraits and history paintings were well-received and he was patronised by the Royal Family.

This and the following almost contemporary engraving are linked by the participation in both of the engraver and miniature painter, Daniel Orme, and by their common subject matter of a meeting between eastern and western dignitaries. In the first, a Turkish ambassador is being presented to the British king; in the second, British naval officers are being welcomed by the Turkish prime minister.

Francis B. Spilsbury (1761-after 1805)
and/or Daniel Orme (c.1766-after 1832)

Meeting in the Grand Vizir's Tent   c.1800

Stipple engraving, coloured by hand, laid down on paper mount
with wash borders
26.5 x 35.8 cm.
Numbered *No 16* and inscribed on mount *See Scott's Life of Napoleon B –
Vol 4. Page 98*

In 1799, in an attempt to extend his influence in Syria, Napoleon
(see p.22) laid siege to Acre. He was repulsed by the Turks whose
land forces were led by the Grand Vizir, Yusuf Diya, with the aid
of the British fleet commanded by Sir William Sidney Smith.
Spilsbury, as Surgeon on *Le Tigre*, a ship of the British fleet,
witnessed this and other actions in the campaign. He was also an
artist and his sketches were later used for publication in his
*Picturesque Scenery In The Holy Land And Syria, Delineated During
The Campaigns Of 1799 and 1800* (1803). This stipple engraving is
one of a set of nineteen preliminary compositions, mostly
watercolours, for this volume; all these are now contained in an

album in the Searight Collection. The respective roles of Spilsbury
and Orme in these watercolours and engravings are not entirely
clear, for, while the two title pages of the album state that the images
are by Spilsbury, the lettering on the plates in the publication states
that they are drawn by Orme after Spilsbury's on-the-spot sketches.

After the naval action, Spilsbury participated in various
reconnoitring trips made by some of the British officers into Syria
and Palestine. In this engraving, Sir Sidney, with two other naval
officers and Spilsbury himself in attendance, is shown participating
in the ceremony during which the Grand Vizir applied his seal to
the *firman* (official pass) authorising their visit to Jerusalem. Their
conversation is aided by an interpreter, and behind them are the
Turkish guard and other officials.

Albert Way FSA (1805-1874)

Interview of the Revd. Lewis Way, with the Emir of Mt. Lebanon. 1823

Watercolour and bodycolour, with gum, on stiff paper
10.7 x 13.6 cm.
Inscribed with title and *at Serayat Bteddin (house of the Law) near Der el Kammar.* and dated *June 14. 1823. 7A.M.*

'... we were conducted to the presence chamber of the Prince. He was seated on his own legs on a low divan; on his right was another, about as high as a sofa, where we were directed to sit. On one side of the divan stood nine pages richly dressed, and on the other, opposite the Prince, a number of military and other officers, the physician, our dragoman, his son, and a few others sitting in the Eastern style on the floor...'.

The Revd Lewis Way's description of his encounter with the Amir Bashir II, ruler of Mount Lebanon, in his splendid palace at Bayt al-Din, is illustrated by his son, Albert, then only eighteen years old, in this colourful and charmingly naive watercolour. Albert had accompanied his father to this meeting in June 1823, during a proposed expedition to Palestine, when, prevented by plague from reaching Jerusalem, they had remained some months in Lebanon, visiting the indomitable Lady Hester Stanhope as well as the awesome Amir.

Richard Dighton (1795-1880)

His Excellency The Persian Ambassador 1819

Etching, coloured by hand
30.3 x 25.4 cm.
Lettered with title in capitals and *Drawn Etchd & Pubd by Richd Dighton May 1819.*

The Turks were not the only Eastern nation to establish diplomatic relations with Britain (see p.90). In 1809-10 Fath Ali Shah of Persia sent Mirza Abul Hasan Shirazi as his 'envoy extraordinary' to England, to seal an alliance between the two countries. Abul Hasan's charm and good looks ensured that within a very short time of his arrival he was lionised by London society as an exotic bird of paradise from a remote and fabulous land: 'the Persian Ambassador is the principal thing talked of now', noted the essayist Charles Lamb. He became the subject of many portraits, including splendid full-length paintings by the two most successful portrait painters of the day, Sir Thomas Lawrence and Sir William Beechey.

Dighton's rather more irreverent portrait of the envoy was published when he arrived for his second visit to London in May 1819. Dressed in his riding habit, he is mounted on a grey Arab stallion. He aroused as much curiosity as before, and his reputation as a ladies' man was enhanced by 'the fair Circassian' who accompanied him. Despite his fame at the time, the image of him that has endured is the less-than-flattering portrayal of him as 'Mirza Firouz', the Persian Ambassador, in James Morier's two picaresque novels about Persia and the Persians, *The Adventures of Hajii Baba of Ispahan* (1824) and *The Adventures of Hajii Baba of Ispahan in England* (1828).

after Constantin Capou-Daghlé (active c.1808)

Sultan Selim III 1808

Stipple engraving printed in black, brown, red and blue,
by Luigi Schiavonetti (1765-1810)
Trimmed to 40.6 x 25.8 cm.
Lettered *Dessiné par Constantin Capou-Daghlé Sujet Ottoman L'année 1808 Gravé par L Schiavonetti à Londres*

Selim III (1789-1807) was one of the most cultured and enlightened of later Ottoman sultans and the first deliberately to put in motion a series of westernising reforms, known collectively as the *Nizam-i Cedid*. Turkish response to these was not generally favourable, and most unpopular were his attempts to improve and modernise the Ottoman army by reorganising it along European lines. The janissaries, the army's most élite and powerful corps, were resentful of this threat to their privileged position, and in 1807 they deposed Selim who was eventually murdered.

Constantin Capou-Daghlé was an artist of Greek origin, possibly from Kapıdaği on the Sea of Marmara in western Turkey, of whom little is known. He may have been Selim's court painter. He was certainly influenced by western artistic traditions, and it is just possible that he may have visited Europe during Selim's reign. The engraver, Schiavonetti, was an Italian, working in London from 1790.

95

after Edouard Riou (1833-1900)

La Tribune Des Souverains   1869

Lithograph with two tint-stones, coloured by hand,
by Jules Didier (1831-1892) and Eugène Ciceri (1813-1890)
25 x 39.5 cm.
Inscribed *Riou*; lettered with title and *Riou pinxt.   Didier et Eug. Ciceri lith*
and *Imp. Lemercier & Cie. Paris.*

Riou's lithograph depicts a significant event in the history of communications between the East and the West. People of different races and creeds are participating together in a religious ceremony held at Port Said to celebrate the inauguration in November 1869 of the Suez Canal, which, by linking the Mediterranean with the Red Sea, created the shortest maritime route connecting Europe to India and the Far East. (See also p.24.)

To mark this historic occasion, Khedive Ismail of Egypt invited a large group of European royalty to attend the ceremonies. These included the Empress Eugénie of France, the Emperor of Austria, the Crown Prince of Prussia, and the Crown Prince and Princess

of the Netherlands. They are shown in this lithograph seated under the vast canopy of the royal tribune with the Khedive and other members of the Egyptian royal family, as well as several other important dignitaries. Riou's lithograph also shows the two tribunes for the religious officials: on the left the bearded and turbaned Muslim leaders, in the centre the white-surpliced Christian prelates. In the background is the newly-built lighthouse of Port Said.

The lithograph is one of twenty in Gustave Nicole's *Inauguration du Canal de Suez. Voyage des Souverains*, published in Paris in 1869 to commemmorate the opening of the Canal. In the same year Riou also published another commemmorative set of lithographs, *Voyage Pittoresque A Travers L'Isthme De Suez*. He contributed to many such publications, and also illustrated books by Jules Verne.

Sir John Tenniel (1820-1914)

Waiting for Relief 1894

Pencil, on card
15.8 x 20.7 cm.
Signed with monogram *JT* and dated *1894*.

Tenniel's superb draughtsmanship is well illustrated in this drawing. It was published in *Punch*, in the issue for 27 January 1894, with the title, *Waiting for Relief*, and captioned, *Turkey. "Hullo! You've all come to it, 'ave you? Why, I've been a Casual for years!"*. It is a parody of Luke Fildes's painting, *Applicants for Admission to a Casual Ward*, exhibited at the Royal Academy twenty years earlier, and satirises the economic and political difficulties that several European countries, including Britain, suffered in 1894.

They are here portrayed as casualties, now forced to join Turkey on the 'sick ward'.

For nearly half a century, Tenniel expressed national attitudes to the major political and social issues of the Victorian age through more than 2000 cartoons published weekly in *Punch*. He also contributed illustrations to many other books and periodicals, the best known being Lewis Carroll's *Alice* stories.

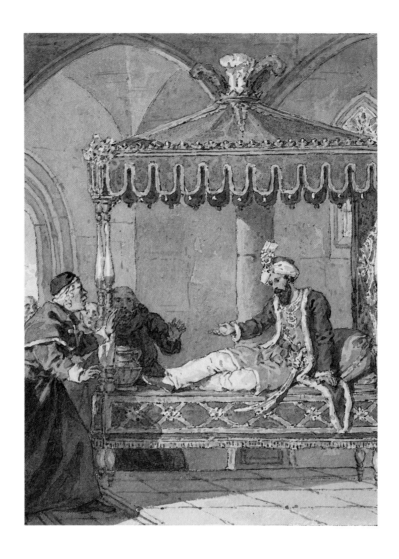

John Augustus Atkinson OWS (1755-after 1833)

A Sultan on a Divan,
giving audience to some Monks   c.1800-20

Ink and watercolour
14.9 x 11.4 cm.
Signed on the back *J.A. Atkinson delt*

This is probably an illustration for a fanciful oriental tale, but the
subject has not been identified. Atkinson illustrated several books,
including *The Miseries of Human Life* (1807) and *Manners . . . of the
Russians* (1812). He also painted battle-pieces, scenes of everyday
life and literary subjects.

SOCIETY
Costumes and Customs; Odalisques and Warriors; Daily Life

For many artists, the people of the Near East were a potent source of inspiration. The enormous range of different racial types, customs and costumes found throughout the Orient is reflected in the diversity of western artists' images. These fluctuated widely in their accuracy, some being founded on direct observation, some being based on other artists' images or on hearsay. Western artists' portrayals of oriental people had a number of different purposes: some were primarily costume figures; some were portraits of identified individuals; some were shown engaged in a particular activity or displaying a local custom; some were seen participating in a specific event, such as a naval or military action; and some were deliberate fantasies.

Until the end of the eighteenth century only a few artists had visited the Near East, and most Europeans' idea of the 'oriental' was that conjured up by the Arabian Nights – a world of voluptuous houris, wonder-working genii, and pagan princes commanding untold riches. This image persisted well into the nineteenth century: it is reflected both in William Thackeray's description of J.F. Lewis's existence in Cairo in the 1840s (see p.131) as 'like a languid Lotus-eater, a dreamy, lazy, hazy, tobaccofied life', and later, in a more extreme form, in Frederick Sandys's fanciful image of *Bhanavar the Beautiful* (p.120). By far the majority of nineteenth-century portrayals of oriental people were more authentic than Sandys's, being the result of first-hand experience. Artists in the first half of the century, like Louis Dupré, Grigoriy Gagarin and William Page (pp.104, 106, 118, 125), certainly focussed on their exotic costumes, aware that their traditional forms of dress were being changed by imported European influences. But even later in the century there was little need to exaggerate, for despite modernisation, the inhabitants everywhere – of the streets, the bazaars, the coffee-houses, the mosques, and the private houses – provided the artist with a wealth of colourful pictorial material.

Costumes and Customs

Godfrey Thomas Vigne FRGS (1801-1863)

Portrait of Abdul Samut Khan   Probably 1836

Watercolour over pencil, on paper watermarked S WISD 1828
23.2 x 21.7 cm.
Signed *G.T.Vigne*, inscribed *Abdul Samud – Persian General in Dost Mohds. Service Kabul* and number *49*; inscribed on the back, probably by Dr.Joseph Wolff, *Nayeb Abdul Samut Khan The Murderer of Colonel Stoddart, Captain Conolly, Captain Wybur[d] Cavalliere Naselli,* and *of Hajèe Muhammad Kokanee – one of the officers of the Sultan of Constantinople*

Vigne was an intrepid explorer and a gifted amateur artist, especially in his powerful characterisation of the various ethnic types he encountered on his travels. His ability to capture the racial and personal individuality of his sitters is exemplified well in the portraits illustrated here and on p.107.

Vigne met Abdul Samut in 1836 at the court of Dost Muhammad, then ruler of Kabul. He took an instant dislike to him, but was persuaded, for his own safety, to give him the bottle of brandy he was demanding. Abdul Samut later moved from Kabul to Bukhara, where he became the right-hand man of the notorious Amir, and was allegedly responsible for numerous cruel activities, including the murder in 1842 of two British officers, Colonel Charles Stoddart and Captain Arthur Conolly. When Dr Joseph Wolff, an indomitable clergyman, attempted to discover what had happened to them, he was imprisoned, and only narrowly avoided the same fate. The story is told in Wolff's *Narrative of a Mission to Bokhara in the years 1843-1845* (2 vols, 1845), where this portrait is reproduced as a lithograph.

Abdool Sumud, Peeghan General to
Dost Mohd's Senior Kabul.

Jost Amman (1539-1591)

A wealthy Turkish woman appearing in public with her children   1577

Woodcut, coloured by hand
23.1 x 17.1 cm.
Lettered *TURCICAE DIVITIS FOEMINAE UNA cum liberis suis in publicum prodeuntis pictura*, with number *CCIIII*, and with descriptive verse in German

This woodcut is one of 219 that illustrated *Habitus praecipuorum populorum, tam virorum quam foeminarum singulari arte depicti*, with a preface by H.Weigel, published in Nuremberg in 1577. Together with twelve others from the series, it is among the items of earliest date in the Searight Collection.

The costume of the figures is remarkably accurate for a time when first-hand knowledge of the Turks was scanty and misconceptions were common. Although the woman's headdress is a fanciful interpretation of a *yaşmak*, and her cloak a westernised version of a *ferace* (sleeved coat), her short-sleeved, patterned *entari* (robe), worn over a long-sleeved *entari* and white *gömlek* (undershirt), are authentic, as are the costumes of the children, except that the boy wears the turban of an adult man.

Amman, who worked mainly in Nuremberg, was a leading woodcut artist and etcher of his day; he also painted portraits and scenes of everyday life, and made designs for stained glass.

TVRCICÆ DIVITIS FOEMINÆ VNA
cum liberis suis in publicum prodeuntis pictura,

CCIIII.
Tracht der reichen Türckischen Weiber/sampt jren Kindern.
WAs reicher Türcken Weiber sindt/   Zu jemandt gehn vber die Gassen/
Wann sie wöllen vnd jre Kindt.   Sindt sie gekleidt in solcher massen.

Anonymous

A Woman with her Son and Daughter, probably Feneriotes   Mid-18th century

Gouache and watercolour touched with white, with gum, on vellum
18.1 x 25 cm.

Another mother with her two children, also a boy and a girl, is here
represented in a gouache painting, two centuries later than
Amman's woodcut (p.102). This image is not one of a series of
costume plates but a portrayal of an actual family (as yet
unidentified) at home in their drawing room, furnished in the
fashionably French style. The boy is dressed as a *dragoman*
(interpreter), probably an indication of his father's profession.
Together with the costume of the mother and daughter, this
suggests that they are Feneriotes, a wealthy group of people of
Greek descent, who lived in the Fener quarter of Constantinople.
The administrative and linguistic talents of the Feneriotes often
brought them into high office in the Ottoman Empire, and during
the eighteenth century they gained virtual control of the trans-
Danubian principalities of Wallachia and Moldavia, satellite states
of the Ottomans.

Louis Dupré (1789-1837)

Un Prince Arménien Et Sa Femme   1825

Lithograph, coloured by hand
34.6 x 25.1 cm.
Lettered with title and *(Duz=Oglou.)*, numbered *XXXIII*, blind-stamped with a circular illegible stamp; also lettered *Dupré delt.   Imp.de Lemercier, Bernard et Cie.*

The woman's costume here is typical of that worn by Turkish women at the time, whether Christian or Muslim. The man's hat suggests that he may be an Armenian from Rumania.

This lithograph is Plate XXXIII from Dupré's *Voyage à Athènes et à Constantinople*, published in Paris in 1825. The volume, consisting of forty plates with text, shows a variety of people and costumes, mainly of Greek origin, and all of them accurately and skilfully drawn. It resulted from the artist's journey to Greece and Constantinople in 1819.

Camille Rogier (1810-1896)

Entering the Bath   1846-48

Lithograph, with one tint-stone, coloured by hand
39.4 x 25.4 cm.
Lettered with title in French, Turkish and English, and *Dess. et lith. par Camille Rogier.   Imprimé par Lemercier, à Paris.* and numbered *29*

Rogier's reputation as an artist was based on his book illustrations, but he also developed a wide range of artistic skills as draughtsman, painter, lithographer, etcher and photographer. A friend of the Orientalist writer Gérard de Nerval, Rogier lived in Constantinople between 1840 and 1843. On his return to Paris he published a volume of lithographs entitled *La Turquie* (1846), illustrating the public and private lives of Turkish people.

The lithograph from the series shown here depicts a group of women entering the *hammam* (bath). The ritual of the *hammam* excited much curiosity in Europe, and was the object of several artists' attention. For Turkish women it was as important an opportunity for social contact as for cleansing. Rogier's women are elegantly wrapped in striped towels; on their feet they wear *nalın* (high wooden clogs), with inlaid mother-of-pearl decoration, to raise them above the wet marble floor. Despite these authentic details, Rogier would not have been permitted to witness the scene.

Prince Grigoriy Grigorievich Gagarin (1810-1893)

A Georgian Man   c.1842

Watercolour and bodycolour, with gum, over pencil
37.9 x 27.1 cm.
Signed in Russian with monogram, inscribed *Georgien (Kakhétie.)*, with costume notes, *No. 2 de la 11e liv[...]* and *28;* inscribed on the back *Georgien [?]*.

The remote and mountainous region of the Caucasus was seldom visited by western travellers in the nineteenth century. Gagarin travelled there in the 1840s, and his studies of its people and scenery were later published as lithographs in two volumes, *Le Caucase pittoresque* (1845–59) and *Scènes, paysages, moeurs et costumes du Caucase* (1850?), both with accompanying text by Count Ernest von Stackelberg. The man shown here appeared in the latter publication, and illustrates superbly Gagarin's accurate observation of the colourful costumes worn by the local people. (See also p.118).

The son of the Russian ambassador to Rome, Gagarin studied art in Italy. He returned to St Petersburg in 1832, and later in the decade went on diplomatic missions to Munich and Constantinople. After visiting the Caucasus he became a respected member of the artistic establishment in St Petersburg, serving as Vice-President of its Academy of Fine Arts, 1859-79.

Godfrey Thomas Vigne FRGS (1801-1863)

The Kuzzelbash of Kabul   1836-39

Pencil, wash and watercolour
20.7 x 16 cm.
Inscribed with title and number *23*, and *Mortazeh Khan Kuzzelbash Servant of Nawab Jubar Khan aged 60. Cabul* and date *16th. July 1839*

The Bride of the Kuzzelbash Kabul

Pencil, wash and watercolour, heightened with white
25.8 x 20.1 cm.
Inscribed with title and number *48*, and *Kabul or Afghan*

Murtaza Khan, the head of a family of the Qizilbash tribe, met Vigne near Ghazni and accompanied him to Kabul. His tough, swarthy features make a striking contrast with the pale skin and meek demeanour of his young and beautiful bride.

The pair of drawings are two of a large group of Persian, Afghan and Indian portraits and landscapes (now mainly in the Searight Collection, the India Office Library and the Royal Geographical Society) that were done by Vigne during his long journey, between 1832 and 1839, through Turkey and Persia to India, and thence northwards to the Western Himalayas and later Afghanistan. (See also p.100.) Vigne published an account of his Afghanistan trip in *A Personal Narrative of a Visit to Ghuzni, Kabul, and Afghanistan* (1840). A further visit made by Vigne to the Near East in 1843-44 is also represented by drawings in the Searight Collection.

Henry William Pickersgill RA (1782-1875)

Three Studies of the Head of a bearded Man wearing a turban

Pencil, touched with white, on blue paper
37.5 x 26.3 cm.
Inscribed with colour notes

Pickersgill exhibited portraits at the Royal Academy for more than sixty years from 1806, and fulfilled many other portrait commissions. A few of these were of oriental subjects, or of Europeans with oriental connections, such as the explorer, James Silk Buckingham. In this fine pencil drawing, the bearded oriental sitter is sensitively characterised in three different poses. Neither his origin nor his identity are known.

Egron Sillif Lundgren (1815-1875)

A Blind Egyptian with a *Madrab* (Teasel) Probably 1860s

Watercolour and bodycolour, with gum, on stiff paper
38.5 x 35.5 cm.

This watercolour is a sympathetic portrayal of a blind Egyptian man seated and holding his *madrab* (teasel), a device for preparing wool and cotton fibres for spinning. Although the men and boys conversing in the background heighten the evocation of an oriental scene, their conviviality also creates a poignant contrast to the lone and silent figure of the blind craftsman, isolated in a world of his own.

Of Swedish origin, Lundgren spent most of his working life abroad. He lived at various times in Italy, Spain and England, and also visited India (with Lord Clyde, 1858-59) and Egypt (1861-62). These two trips to the East supplied him with material for many of his subsequent watercolour paintings. He exhibited these frequently at the Old Water-Colour Society in London between 1862 and 1875.

Alfred Hassam (active 1860s)

Man in Arab Costume, seated and smoking a *çubuk*   Probably 1860s

Watercolour and gum over pencil, touched with white; on top layer of artist's sketching block, the rest of which was formerly retained as a support
25.4 x 17.8 cm.

This may be a portrait of one of the artist's friends or patrons who visited the Near East. His costume was probably assembled in the studio from pieces brought back from the Holy Land. Little is known about Hassam; he was a painter, and a designer of stained-glass windows, who worked mainly in Birmingham. During the 1860s he also exhibited in London. This watercolour shows some influence from the Pre-Raphaelites, although no direct link with any member of that group has been established.

William Charles Thomas Dobson RA RWS (1817-1898)

A Girl with a Fan   1864

Watercolour and gouache
31.4 x 23.6 cm.
Signed with monogram *WCTD* and dated *1864*

Dobson went to Italy in 1845, and spent several years there and in Germany, where he was influenced by the Nazarenes, a group of painters who aimed to regenerate religious art. On his return to England he specialised in religious themes, hoping to revive popular interest in them. He also painted less weighty subjects, a favourite type being exemplified by the idealised portrait of a young girl illustrated here, which a contemporary described as displaying 'a roundness and sweetness, which is never sensual'. Dobson is not known to have visited the Near East, but like several other artists at the time attempted to create a realistic effect with authentic accoutrements, put together in the studio. The girl wears a turban, and a striped silk brocade robe of a type common throughout the Levant during the nineteenth century, but both were worn by men rather than women.

Mariano Fortuny y Marsal (1838-1874)

Study of a Moroccan Man with a Green Wrap   1860s

Watercolour
25.2 x 14.3 cm.
Signed and inscribed *Forty   Roma*

Fortuny studied painting in Barcelona but went to Italy at the age of twenty. After visits to Morocco in 1860 and 1862 he painted numerous oriental subjects, which were much admired for their rich colours and bravura brushwork. Many young French and Italian Orientalist painters were inspired by his work.

This study is an example of Fortuny's rapid but deft manipulation of colour and light. It may relate to a figure in his etching of 1866, *Arabe Veillant Le Corps De Son Ami,* but is also comparable in style to another watercolour dated 1869 (Museo del Prado, Madrid).

William Wiehe Collins RI (1862-1951)

North African Man in travelling costume
c.1890-1910

Watercolour with gum, heightened with white, over pencil, on stiff paper
22.4 × 14.1 cm.
Signed *W Collins*

The rich clothes and proud stance of this African man suggest that he was an attendant in a wealthy household. His fez, of the type known as a *chechia*, his patterned jacket and his cloak, are typical of those worn in Tunis.

Collins painted a variety of subjects, including landscapes, architecture, costume studies and military scenes, and exhibited these widely in London. During the First World War he served in the Dardanelles and Egypt.

Arthur Trevor Haddon RBA **(1864-1941)**

Two Arabs in a Quffa   Possibly 1890-1910

Watercolour, heightened with white, over pencil
25.2 x 35.4 cm.
Inscribed in ball-point pen on the back of the old mount, *by Trevor Haddon*

The two young men are paddling a *quffa*, the traditional circular
boat in use on the Tigris and Euphrates rivers in Mesopotamia.
Their long striped wrap-over robes, and headdresses with heavy
rope-like bands holding the head-cloth in place, were worn at the
turn of the century in southern Arabia, but are now obsolete.
Haddon painted portraits and scenes of everyday life; he also
illustrated books. He is known to have visited Spain and Italy in
the 1880s and 1890s, and to have travelled in North and South
America in the 1920s, but no trip to Mesopotamia is recorded.
It is possible that this scene was based on a photograph.

Odalisques

after Philippe Jacques De Loutherbourg RA
(1740-1812)

A Sultana   1777

Etching and stipple, printed in red, by Gabriel Scorodomoff (c.1748-1792)
31.1 x 34.5 cm.
Lettered with title in capitals and with lines of verse; also
P. J. Loutherbourgh pinxit. G. Scorodomooff Sculpsit. and *London, Printed
for R.Sayer & J.Bennett, Map & Printsellers, No 53 Fleet Street; as the Act directs,
8th Octr 1777.*

De Loutherbourg's 'odalisque', playing with her pet parrot as she
reclines in her luxurious boudoir, exemplifies the mid-eighteenth-
century craze for 'turquerie'. Many ladies of fashion posed for their
portraits *en sultane*, wearing baggy pantaloons, flowing robes and
elaborate turbans, in surroundings intended to evoke an aura of a
Turkish seraglio. The parrot was a familiar symbol in Indian and

Persian love poetry. Interestingly, this print was used as the source
for an early nineteenth-century Mughal painting by an unknown
artist, probably from Lucknow (Chester Beatty Library, Dublin).
With its pair, *A Lady, Contemplating on her Lovers Picture* (another
stipple engraving after a painting by Angelica Kauffmann), *A
Sultana* was intended as decoration for a boudoir or bedroom.

De Loutherbourg came to London from Paris in 1771. He was an
immensely versatile artist. Many of his paintings dealt with
dramatic events, such as battles, shipwrecks, storms, fires and
avalanches, but he also depicted calmer subjects, such as pastoral
scenes and landscapes. His involvement in the theatre was
considerable, particularly as a stage designer. He was also active
as a print-maker and experimented with a variety of techniques.
The engraver, Scorodomoff (or Skorodumov), was a Russian artist
from St Petersburg who was in London during 1775-82.

Thomas Allom FRIBA (1804-1872)

The Favourite Odalisque   Probably 1838-40

Watercolour over pencil
29.6 x 21.4 cm.

'The odalique is a fair slave of Circassia or Georgia, the purchase
and property of her master alone, and frequently the favourite of
his heart – the "light of his harem;" '. So wrote Emily Reeve, the
author of the description accompanying the lithograph of this
watercolour, which was included in Allom's *Character and Costume
in Turkey and Italy*, published by Fisher, probably in 1840.

The image of fair-skinned and elegantly attired ladies in the exotic
surroundings of an oriental harem was a constant theme in
Orientalist painting of the nineteenth century. Allom's
interpretation of the subject is predictably idealised, but the
costumes are nevertheless authentic. The odalisque wears long
baggy trousers (*şalvar*) underneath a long robe with trailing sleeves
(*üçetek),* with a draped shawl girdle (*kuşak*) round her waist; her
hair is elaborately dressed. The composition was undoubtedly
popular, and had earlier been reproduced as an engraving in
another of Fisher's publications, *Constantinople and the Seven
Churches of Asia Minor* (Vol.II, 1839). (See also p.57.)

Henri Félix Emmanuel Philippoteaux (1815-1884)

An Odalisque playing with a Child
Probably 1835-45

Pencil and watercolour, heightened with white
17.8 x 25.5 cm.
Signed *F Philippoteaux* and numbered *No 72* on the mount

Philippoteaux's odalisque lies firmly within the western tradition
of idealised oriental beauty. Stretched out on a rug in the harem,
dallying with her child, she epitomises the indolence and sensuality
that most westerners believed constituted the greater part of the
eastern way of life.

The artist was best known for his military subjects and portraits,
and he exhibited at the Salon in Paris and the Royal Academy in
London. This watercolour may have been done at about the same
time as he contributed illustrations to L.A.Berbrugger's *Algérie
Historique, Pittoresque et Monumentale* (3 vols, 1843-45).

117

Achille-Constant-Théodore-Émile Prisse d'Avennes (1807-1879)

A Nubian Girl standing beside the First Cataract of the Nile   c.1839

Watercolour over pencil, laid down on card watermarked *J WHATMAN 1839*
30.1 x 21.9 cm.

Prisse d'Avennes (p.23) probably journeyed up the Nile on several occasions in the company of travellers who commissioned watercolours of local scenes from him. It seems that he saw girls like the one depicted here, since a similar figure appears in the lithograph *Nubian Females; Kanoosee Tribe. Philae*, published in *Oriental Album* (1848). He must also have been aware that her short skirt and hair-style resemble those of the Nubian dancing girls depicted in Ancient Egyptian reliefs. The whole scene is a delightful *capriccio* in which Prisse has brought together a variety of Egyptian components: as well as the girl with her wicker basket, there is a Nile cataract, a Roman gravestone inscribed in Latin, an ancient Egyptian stone block inscribed with hieroglyphs, and even some typical local flora and fauna.

Prince Grigoriy Grigorievich Gagarin (1810-1893)

A *Bayadère* from Shemakha (Azerbaijan)   c.1842

Watercolour and bodycolour over pencil
38.3 × 27.6 cm.
Inscribed *Bayadere de Chemakha,* with notes on costume colour and details, and *No 64*

The *bayadères* (dancing girls) of Shemakha were famous for their grace and beauty, and for the sensuality of their dancing. Their costume, too, was alluring, consisting, as seen here, of a pair of voluminous trousers, worn with a bodice and tight-fitting jackets, decorated with tassels and a necklace of gold coins, Gagarin's watercolour seems to have been considered too *risqué* for publication in either of his two volumes (see p.106.)

Frederick Sandys (1829-1904)

Bhanavar The Beautiful   1894

Watercolour and bodycolour, over pencil
30.8 x 20.1 cm.

This dramatic image of a woman dancing amidst writhing serpents
was designed to illustrate George Meredith's *The Story of Bhanavar
the Beautiful*, one of a collection of pseudo-oriental tales entitled *The
Shaving of Shagpat, an Arabian Entertainment* (first edition, 1856).
Bhanavar was the beautiful, innocent daughter of a Caucasian *amir*,
who, having gained possession of the magic jewel (seen here
adorning her forehead), became an evil Queen of the Serpents.

The original monochrome version was commissioned from Sandys
in 1864 by the publishers Chapman and Hall as the frontispiece for
their second edition of the tales (1865). This watercolour, the second
version, was painted by Sandys at Meredith's request, for him to
present to a friend. It was reproduced in *The Artist,* Winter Number,
1896, and was also exhibited at the Royal Academy's Winter
Exhibition in 1905.

Book illustration formed a major part of Sandys's output. He
contributed to several contemporary magazines, as well as to
picture books and to editions of poetry, ballads, myths and legends.
Originating in Norwich, he worked in London from 1851, where
he was influenced by the Pre-Raphaelites, particularly Dante
Gabriel Rossetti and his images of luxuriant female figures.

Warriors

William Heath (pseudonym 'Paul Pry') (1795-1840)

A Group of Eastern figures sitting and standing at the entrance to a Tent   1819

Watercolour and bodycolour, with gum, over pencil
38.1 x 27.1 cm.
Signed and dated *William Heath 1819*

This is probably an illustration to an oriental tale or poem, but the subject has not yet been identified. The men at the entrance to the tent appear to be parleying or striking a bargain over something. Their costumes and weaponry are predominantly Indo-Persian, but the scene is more fanciful than authentic, and creates an opportunity for a display of colourful and exotic objects.

Heath, as 'Paul Pry', was one of the most successful caricaturists of the Regency era. He is best known for his *Pickwickian Illustrations* (1837). Earlier, his illustrations had included military subjects, some with a vaguely oriental veneer, such as those to his own poem *The Life of a Soldier* (1823).

Jean-Baptiste Le Prince (1734-1781)

Officier des Janissaires Polonais   1771

Etching and aquatint, printed in brown
Trimmed to 20.2 x 15.6 cm.
Signed and dated *Le Prince 1771 –* ; lettered with title

As a result of his travels in Russia and nearby countries, around
1758, Le Prince published many series of etchings and aquatints
with Russian subjects, such as *Divers Ajustements Et Usages De
Russie* (1763-65). This figure and a companion, a soldier of the same
'Polish Janissaries', are further examples of his interest in Eastern
Europe. Although the Ottoman Empire never extended to Poland,
certain Turkish-style garments were traditionally worn by nobles
and officers until the early nineteenth century. There were also
Polish recruits in Constantinople among the janissaries, the élite
corps in the Ottoman army.

Various experiments using tonal effects had previously been made,
but Le Prince was the first to develop the true aquatint process
using a resin ground, during the 1760s. Here he exploits the fluency
of the medium to express the swaggering pose of the officer and
the violent action of the siege taking place in the background.

Jean-Baptiste Hilair (or Hilaire) (1753-1822)

Albanian Soldier   1778

Pen and ink and watercolour, over pencil
19.4 x 12.8 cm.
Signed and dated *hilaire 1778.;* inscribed illegibly on the back

Hilair's artistic debt to J.B.Le Prince, whose pupil he had been, is
clearly seen in the fine pen outlines and delicate shading of this
drawing.

Hilair was one of several artists employed by the comte de Choiseul-
Gouffier, the French ambassador in Constantinople, 1784-92 (see
also p.36). He had accompanied the comte on an earlier visit to
Greece and Turkey in 1776-79, and contributed numerous
illustrations to his publication *Voyage Pittoresque de la Grèce* (Vol.1,
1782). The drawing illustrated here was made during this journey,
but it was not reproduced. The volume does include a group of
Albanian soldiers in similar attire (Vol.1, Pl.2), and one figure in a
similar stance (Vol 1, Pl.59).

Revd Cooper Willyams (1762-1816)

The first day's attack on the Castle of Aboukir by the Turkish Gun-boats   1798

Watercolour
21.8 x 36.2 cm.
Inscribed with title and *having five British, and five Russian seamen in each, and assisted by the boats of the Swiftsure, octr. 24th. 1798.   on the right, is the wreck of the brig, behind which, the Turkish comman-ders retired during the action, to smoke their pipes.*

Willyams, ordained curate in 1784, served as chaplain on board the *Swiftsure*, one of Nelson's ships in the British campaign against Napoleon in the Mediterranean, 1798-1801 (see p.92). This watercolour is one of five in the Searight Collection reproduced as aquatints in Willyams's publication, *A Voyage up the Mediterranean in His Majesty's Ship the Swiftsure* (1802). Napoleon had invaded Egypt in July 1798, and established himself in Cairo; however, in October that year his fleet was sunk by Nelson's forces off Abu Qir. In his watercolours Willyams shows less interest in the naval action than in the people taking part in it and in scenes of local life. Here, the battle has been relegated to the background, while attention is focussed on the amusing incident in the foreground of the Turkish captains retiring to a small boat in the shelter of a wreck to smoke their pipes.

123

Alexander (Aleksander Ossipovitch) Orlowsky (or Orlovski) (1777-1832)

A Zombarek Firing 1820-21

Lithograph, by Charles-Joseph Hullmandel (1789-1850), coloured by hand
14.7 x 20 cm.
Lettered with title and *Orlowsky ex.nat.del.* and *On stone by C.Hullmandel.;*
also lettered *London. Published by Rodwell & Martin New Bond St.Dec.1.1820.
Printed by C.Hullmandel.*

A *zamburaki* was an infantry soldier.

Although he was born in Warsaw, Orlowski spent most of his
career in Russia. In 1812 he was appointed Court Painter in St
Petersburg, as well as draughtsman to the Department of Military
Topography. He was probably the first artist to practise lithography
in Russia. The lithograph shown here is one of a series published
in four volumes in 1820-21 under the title *Costume of Persia*. This
and other publications on Persia suggest that he may have visited
the country in about 1817-18.

William Page (1794-1872)

A *Mamluk* from Aleppo c.1810-c.1823

Watercolour, touched with white, over pencil
37.7 x 26.4 cm.
Inscribed on the back *Aleppo. Mameluke*

Mamluks were originally slaves imported from the Caucasus who
were educated by their Muslim masters and granted freedom in
return for military service. The individual illustrated here is
portrayed in full ceremonial dress, with loose trousers (*şalvar*), and
shirt with long slashed cuffs (*gömlek*), worn underneath a knee-
length coat woven with a spotted design; his elaborate sash holds
his purse and weapons. He carries his lance in one hand, and in
the other the end of a rope presumably attached to his horse.

This is one of twenty-one costume figure studies by Page in the
Searight Collection, which show Ottoman and other Near Eastern
characters of various ranks and occupations, both male and female.
Page recorded in great detail their exotic and colourful costumes in
the years immediately preceding the modernising reforms that
gradually eroded many traditional forms of dress and behaviour.
Some of his figures were already anachronistic. (See also p.74.)

Alexandre-Gabriel Decamps (1803-1860)

Albanian Duel

Watercolour and bodycolour, with gum, heightened with white
30 x 39.6 cm.
Signed *Decamps* and inscribed on the old mount ALBANIAN DUEL By DESCAMPS

The Albanians, dressed in flowing garments and renowned for their aggressive temperament, were a favourite subject with Romantic artists. In this watercolour, Decamps has focussed on the tension between the two combatants as they glare fiercely at one another and parry with their rapiers, each goading the other on while their cloaks and white skirts (*fustán*) swirl around them. The drama is echoed by the men and galloping horses approaching from the background.

Decamps's oriental subjects resulted from a trip to Greece, Albania and Turkey in 1827-28. When they were exhibited at the Salon from 1831 onwards, they were highly acclaimed, and in his lifetime he became almost as famous as Eugène Delacroix.

Carl Haag RWS (1820-1915)

War 1871

Watercolour, on thick paper
51.9 x 36.8 cm.
Inscribed with title, signed and dated *Carl Haag 1871*.

Haag (see p.42) continued to paint predominantly Oriental subjects for many years after his visit to the Near East in 1858-60. This watercolour, and its companion, *Peace* (whereabouts unknown), are two such examples, painted shortly before his return visit to Egypt in 1873. The wounded drummer-boy is borne back to camp on his camel, and the nearby battle is further indicated by the assorted weapons carried by the two soldiers. Haag may also have intended to point a contrast between the young Nubian boy in his uniform of a *nizam,* or new-style regular soldier in the Egyptian army, and the older Arnavut (Albanian), many of whom had formerly been employed as irregular mercenaries.

War

Carl Haag 1871.

127

Auguste Delacroix (1809-1868)

A Moroccan Amir   1850

Watercolour and bodycolour, with gum, over pencil,
on paper watermarked *J WHATMAN*
42 x 27.3 cm.
Inscribed and dated *Tangier. 1850,* and signed *A.Delacroix.;*
numbered *44* on former mount

Another military personality, different in time and place, is seen
here, also sumptuously, though less elaborately, attired than
Page's (p.124). Delacroix's gallant captain stands proudly in
brilliant sunshine within the walls of the Citadel of Tangier, his
martial position further emphasised by the cannon in the
background. Portrayed in profile, his hawk-like features and alert,
watchful stance are distinctive.

Auguste Delacroix (not to be confused with his more famous
namesake) became known for his scenes of everyday rural and
coastal life set in and around his native Boulogne. Half-way
through his career, in about 1849-50, he visited Morocco, and
thereafter oriental subjects were included among the paintings he
exhibited at the Salon. This watercolour must have been painted
during or shortly after his visit to Tangier.

Louis-Eugène Ginain (1818-1886)

Marche d'Infanterie en Algérie   c.1843

Watercolour and bodycolour, heightened with white, over pencil;
cut across at the top corners
27.3 x 23.3 cm.
Signed *Eug.Ginain;* inscribed on former mount with title and *Eug:Ginain.*

This appears to depict an episode in the French army's capture in
1843 of the retinue of Abd al-Qadir, leader of Algerian resistance
to French colonialism. After the loss of his women and slaves, it
was said by a contemporary French historian that the great Algerian
chieftain was no longer a man: he surrendered in 1847, thus
completing French hegemony in Algeria. The most famous
representation of the event was Horace Vernet's huge *Prise de la
Smala d'Abd-el-Kader par le duc d'Aumale,* painted in 1845 as part of
the decoration of the Galerie des Batailles at Versailles.

Ginain exhibited frequently at the Salon in Paris and was known
for his paintings of military subjects, which, after a visit to Algeria
in 1840, included scenes from the French conquest.

William Wyld RI (1806-1889)

Marchand de Legumes à Alger   1833-35

Watercolour with touches of bodycolour, and with gum
26.4 x 19.6 cm.
Signed *W.Wyld.*; inscribed with title on the back; inscribed *William Wyld (boutique a Alger.)* on the original mount

Wyld visited Algeria in 1833 and painted several vibrant watercolours of *suqs*, streets and cafés. In the example illustrated here he exploits the rich pictorial potential of the different colours, shapes and textures of the locally-produced objects on display. The seated shop-keeper in Turkish dress, surrounded by his wares, provides a focal point for the composition.

Like his compatriot, Richard Parkes Bonington, Wyld received lessons in watercolour from Louis Francia; all three can be described as Anglo-French artists, their careers divided between the two countries. Wyld was also influenced by the Orientalist artist Horace Vernet, whom he met in Algeria and to whom he dedicated his series of lithographs, *Voyage pittoresque dans la Régence d'Alger exécuté en 1833*, published in collaboration with Emile Lessore in Paris in 1835. The watercolour shown here is reproduced as one of these lithographs, entitled *Marchand de la Rue de Chartres*.

John Frederick Lewis RA (1805-1876)

Scene in a Cairo Bazaar   1856

Watercolour and bodycolour, heightened with white
45.5 x 59.6 cm.
Signed and dated *J.F.Lewis 1856*

Lewis's understanding of Egyptian life is well shown in this watercolour. A storyteller or poetry-reciter is performing, with musical accompaniment from a *rabab* (a kind of viol), to a crowd of passers-by. He holds up his forefinger and thumb either in a gesture to reinforce a point in his story or to display a small object – a coin or jewel – to his audience. They listen with rapt attention – men and women, young and old, fair and dark, rich and poor, representative of the medley of different types of people found in Cairo's busy streets. Among them are a wealthy merchant with his two wives and servant, whose garments create an opportunity for Lewis to display his knowledge of local costume and his skill in

rendering the texture and sheen of rich materials. The street is the Sharia Bab al-Wazir, identifiable from the dome of the Mosque of Amir Khayrbak in the background.

Lewis arrived in Cairo in late 1841 and spent the following decade there living as an Ottoman Turk in an old Mamluk house. He returned to England in 1851 with a large collection of sketches on which he based his highly acclaimed watercolour and oil paintings. The watercolour illustrated here, dated 1856, appears to have been a private commission, since it was not exhibited. (See also p.78.)

Henry Pilleau RI (1813-1899)

Scene in an Egyptian Town   1869

Watercolour and bodycolour, heightened with white, over pencil,
on blue/grey paper
25.2 x 35.3 cm.
Signed with monogram and dated *HP 1869.*

Egyptian men and women are seen here in a town or village on the
Nile. In the shade of an overhanging tree a market stall displays its
wares, including paper lanterns and bread. At the stall behind,
sugar cane is for sale. In the background is a mosque with a
white minaret, though not distinctive enough to establish the
scene's locality.

Pilleau had visited Egypt in the winter of 1842-43 with Lieutenant-
Colonel George Everest (after whom Mount Everest was named)
and two other companions, on their way home from India. On his
return to England he published a set of twelve coloured lithographs,
Sketches in Egypt (1845), which, like the better-known publications
of Wilkie, Roberts and Owen Jones in the same decade, fuelled
popular interest in Egypt and the Holy Land. The success of his
work may have encouraged him to give up his army career in order
to devote his time to painting and travelling. He visited Egypt
again in 1863 and 1868-69, and exhibited, at several London
institutions, scenes of rural and urban life in this and other
countries.

Andrew Carrick Gow RA RI (1848-1920)

Village Men conversing with Two Armed Horsemen, Algiers   1884

Watercolour and bodycolour, on board
35.7 x 51.7 cm.
Signed and dated *A.C.Gow   1884*

The men are conversing outside a small house near the Fontaine du Hamma and the Café des Platanes on the outskirts of Algiers; perhaps they are striking a bargain over the basket of oranges at their feet. The composition may be the same or similar to one entitled *Algerian Gossip,* exhibited by Gow at the Royal Academy in 1886. It is not known whether Gow visited Algeria and witnessed the scene himself, or whether he based it on a photograph or other image.

Gow painted a variety of subjects, which he exhibited mainly at the New Water-Colour Society, but also at the Royal Academy, where he became Keeper and Librarian in 1911.

Carl Goebel (1824-1899)

View of Belgrade, with the ruin of the Gate of Prince Eugène of Savoy   Probably 1860s

Watercolour, with gum, heightened with white, over pencil
34.5 x 58 cm.
Inscribed *vue de Belgrad   la ruine du Prince Eugene*
and signed *C Goebel*.

Belgrade, the capital of Serbia, was under Ottoman rule until the
early nineteenth century, and a Turkish garrison remained in the
fortress until 1867. The watercolour illustrated here shows a street
in which different ethnic types are represented. The Christian
Serbs include two women in traditional Serb costume with their
elaborate headdresses, a youth, and a man wearing a brown cloak
and fur hat. Among the Muslim Turks are two men conversing,
possibly Ottoman officials; some women in their usual outdoor
dress with *yaşmaks* covering their heads, making purchases from
a street vendor; and an old man, seated with crossed legs, watching
life go by. In the background looms the gaunt ruin of the Gate of
Prince Eugène of Savoy, part of the Small Kalemegdan or fortress
of Belgrade. The Gate was built in 1717 to commemorate the
Austrian victory over the Turks that year.

Goebel was an Austrian watercolourist and lithographer who
specialised in landscapes and scenes of local life. He travelled
widely, visiting Belgrade in the 1860s.

Amadeo Preziosi, Fifth Count (1816-1882)

A Turkish Coffee House, Constantinople   1854

Pencil and watercolour, heightened with white
40.7 x 58.8 cm.
Signed and dated *Preziosi 1854.* and inscribed on the back *In Constantinople*

This is a fine example of Preziosi's keen observation of
contemporary Turkish life, seen here in a lively scene, rapidly
sketched yet full of accurately depicted detail (see also p.70). A
large gallery of characters is portrayed, all of them evidence of the
cosmopolitan character of Constantinople. On the left can be seen
a *saz* (group of musicians); a Greek with a *çubuk* (long, cherry-wood
pipe) and a negro lad applying a glowing piece of charcoal to the
bowl, carrying at the same time a *narghile* (water-pipe); as well as
a Mevlavi or whirling dervish in his distinctive *külâh* (felt hat). In
the background are merchants, including a Persian. In the

foreground is another merchant with a *çubuk*, and at the door an
unveiled beggar-woman on her rounds. To their right are a
Circassian with cartridges on the front of his coat, and two more
Greeks smoking. The coffee-house itself is a luxurious nineteenth-
century Baroque structure, probably on the shore of the Golden
Horn. Equipment is clearly shown: on the left a row of *narghiles*
with some spare tubes and a large water-pot; behind them, in the
corner, the stove for heating the coffee and the charcoal for the
pipes. Next to the Greek in the right foreground are a coffee-cup
and its metal holder. In the centre is an elaborate fountain, which
cooled the room in summer.

135

after Sir David Wilkie RA (1785-1841)

The Turkish Courier relating the News
of the capture of Acre   1843

Lithograph, with two tint-stones, by Joseph Nash ows
(1809-1878), coloured by hand
32.4 x 38.8 cm.
Inscribed with title, and signed, inscribed and dated
D Wilkie f Constantinople   1840

Sir David Wilkie RA (1785-1841)

Sketch for *The Tartar Messenger Narrating the News of the Victory of St.Jean d'Acre*   1840

Pencil, pen and brown ink
31.7 x 24.4 cm.
Numbered *No 28*
On the back, a preliminary pencil sketch, probably for the same subject

Wilkie was in Constantinople when news came of the Anglo-Turkish victory over the Egyptians at St Jean d'Acre (Acre, Syria) on 4 November 1840. The excitement of the event inspired one of the few oils painted (though not finished) during his sojurn in the Near East. The sketch shown here is a study for it; the lithograph of the same scene is Plate 25 of the twenty-six published after Wilkie's death as *Sir David Wilkie's Sketches in Turkey, Syria & Egypt, 1840 & 1841. Drawn on Stone by Joseph Nash* (1843). In both compositions the men surrounding the courier listen eagerly, their pipes forgotten, as he narrates the events of the battle, no doubt embellished in the telling. In the lithograph, the barber on the left pays scant attention to the chin he is shaving and only the two little girls, introduced by Wilkie as a contrast to the men, are oblivious of the drama. The event takes place in a café, and although several races are represented (including Turkish, Armenian and Jewish), few subsidiary details are introduced – unlike the café scene by Preziosi (p.135) – so as not to detract from the tension of the central episode.

Wilkie, who had already established a high reputation as a painter of Scottish rural life, and latterly of more topical events, was in the Near East to study real settings and people for the biblical subjects that he hoped to paint on his return. His hopes were never realised owing to his untimely death at sea on the journey home in 1841.

Gustavo Simoni (1846-1926)

Une Caravane en Repos en Kabylie   1885

Watercolour over pencil, on thick paper
37.4 x 54.4 cm.
Signed and dated *G.Simoni.1885.*; on old label formerly attached to the
frame inscribed with title, *No 2,* and *G.Simone c/o A Brébant 74 Rue
D'Amsterdam Paris*

Simoni was a leading member of the group of Italian Orientalists based in Rome in the late nineteenth century. He first visited North Africa in 1877-79, and afterwards returned to Algeria several times. In this watercolour he has depicted the halt of a caravan of travellers from the Berber and other African tribes in the Kabylia region of Algeria. While the men have been travelling on foot or riding on camels, the women sit together in covered litters precariously perched on other camels' backs. The presence of both dark and pale-skinned faces reflects the mixture of different races contained within these tribes. The posed figures suggest that Simoni may well have used a photograph as an *aide-memoire* for his detailed composition. It appears to have been a success, for in the same year he made a larger oil version of it, which differs only in minor details (formerly with the Mathaf Gallery, London).

ANIMALS

Jean-Baptiste Adanson (1732-1804)

Rat d'Egypte apellé en Arabe Gérbouh
1775-c.1800

Watercolour over pencil
29.5 x 46.5 cm.
Lettered with title

Jerboas are well adapted to their life in the arid desert. Renowned for their cunning, they are mainly nocturnal, emerging from their burrows to forage for food in the evening. Their tufted tails, longer than the head and body combined, help them to balance as they leap tremendous distances on their strong back legs. The Lesser Egyptian Jerboa *(Jaculus jaculus)* is found throughout Egypt. During the Second World War its common name, Desert Rat, was adopted as a nickname by the British Eighth Army.

Adanson was French Consul in Egypt, 1775-85, several years before the Napoleonic invasion. During this time he filled many sketch-books and portfolios with drawings of the flora and fauna, antiquities, and landscape of the country. This delightful watercolour was made either during his sojourn in Egypt or afterwards, in the 1790s, when publication of his material was proposed, though was never finally realised.

Etched by Js.Gillray, from the Original Intercepted Drawing.

James Gillray (1756/7-1815)

"L'Insurrection de l'Institut Amphibie."
The Pursuit of Knowledge. 1799

Etching, coloured by hand
25.2 x 35.6 cm.
Lettered with title and *Etched by Js.Gillray, from the Original Intercepted Drawing.* and *Pubd March 12th. 1799. by – H.Humphrey St James s Street*

Gillray satirises the efforts of Napoleon's Institut d'Égypte, established in August 1798, to impose French civilisation on Egypt. Their hostile reception is here illustrated: Egypt in the form of a ferocious crocodile has turned on the man who has attempted to harness it, while his training manual, *Sur L'Education du Crocodile,* lies in pieces on the ground; in the background, a second 'trainer' tries to escape from the jaws of another hungry crocodile. This

etching is the second of a set of seven published by H.Humphrey in 1799 as *Egyptian Sketches,* and one of many caricatures by Gillray of various episodes in Napoleon's expedition to Egypt and Palestine in 1798-99. (See also pp.22, 92 & 123.)

Gillray's cruel wit picked on almost every political and social issue of the day, not least the Napoleonic Wars. He was a master of the art of caricature, and his hand-coloured etchings were supreme not only for their biting irony and fertile imagery, but also for their technical virtuosity.

The Tents Gebel el Checkop
W. Cairo Feby 20th 1864.

Elijah Walton (1832-1880)

Study of a Camel's Head   1864

Black chalk, on pale green paper
22.4 x 29.5 cm.
Inscribed and dated *The Tents Gebel el Checkop[?] W.Cairo Feby 20th 1864.*

Walton was in Egypt a good deal during the 1860s, and made many
drawings and watercolours of its people and landscape. He
developed a special interest in the ubiquitous camel, and in
1863-64 spent time in a Bedouin encampment near Cairo studying
the animal's habits and anatomy. The following year he published
his drawings in *The Camel, its Anatomy, Proportions and Paces*,
comparable in its detail and accuracy to Stubbs's *Anatomy of the
Horse*, of almost exactly a century earlier.

Walton was also known as a painter of romantic Alpine landscapes.
He exhibited these, and oriental subjects, at several London
institutions, and published some of them in *Vignettes: Alpine And
Eastern* (1873).

Frederick Goodall RA (1822-1904)

A Female Riding Camel 1893

Watercolour, heightened with white, over pencil
27.3 x 38.9 cm.
Signed with monogram and dated *FG 1893*

Camels were used for a variety of domestic purposes throughout Egypt. Some, like the baggage camel depicted in a companion watercolour to the one shown here (also in the Searight Collection), were bred for their strength and stamina, and were capable of carrying heavy loads long distances across the desert. The more slender type seen in this watercolour was faster and better suited for riding. She therefore carries a saddle, and her master's dagger and decorated woollen saddle-bag.

Goodall was a prolific and successful Orientalist painter. He first visited Egypt in 1858-59. He shared a house in Cairo with Carl Haag (see p.42 & 126), and they made many sketches together in the streets, outside the city around the Pyramids, and also near Suez. During the 1860s Goodall used these for several carefully constructed paintings of rural and urban Egyptian life and of Biblical scenes. When he visited Egypt again in 1870-71 he lived at Saqqarah, a few miles south of Cairo, so that he could observe the daily life of the Bedouin. In England for the next three decades he continued to paint variations on the same themes as before.

143

Howard Carter (1874-1939)

A Pair of White Pelicans   1899

Watercolour heightened with white
42.1 x 33 cm.
Signed and dated *Howard Carter.   1899*

Many visitors to Egypt drew or commented on the number and
variety of its birds. Among them – as well as Carter (see p.34) – was
Edward Lear, artist, traveller, nonsense writer, and, in his early
career, ornithological draughtsman. One species – the Pelican –
inspired one of his most famous nonsense poems, *The Pelican
Chorus* (1877):

> *We live on the Nile. The Nile we love.*
> *By night we sleep on the cliffs above;*
> *By day we fish, and at eve we stand*
> *On long bare islands of yellow sand.*

Select Bibliography

General:

Yehoshua Ben-Arieh, *The Rediscovery of the Holy Land in the Nineteenth Century*, Jerusalem/Detroit, 1979.

Blue Guides, London/New York: John Freely, *Istanbul*, 1983; Kay Prag, *Jerusalem*, 1988; Veronica Seton-Williams and Peter Stocks, *Egypt*, 1983.

Auguste Boppe, *Les Peintres Du Bosphore au dix-huitième siecle*, Paris, 1911; revised and illustrated edition by Catherine Boppe, Paris, 1989.

Peter Clayton, *The Rediscovery of Ancient Egypt Artists and Travellers in the 19th Century*, London, 1982.

Caroline Juler, *Les Orientalistes de L'Ecole Italienne*, Paris, 1987.

Philippe Jullian, *The Orientalists European Painters of Eastern Scenes*, Oxford, 1977.

Jennifer Scarce, *Women's Costume of the Near and Middle East*, London, 1987.

Sarah Searight, *The British in the Middle East*, London, 1969; revised edition, London, 1979.

Lynne Thornton, *The Orientalists Painter-Travellers 1928-1908*, Paris, 1983.

Lynne Thornton, *Women as Portrayed in Orientalist Painting*, Paris, 1985.

Fani-Maria Tsigakou, *The Rediscovery of Greece Travellers and Painters of the Romantic Era*, London, 1981.

Exhibition Catalogues:

Amman, Jordan National Gallery, *On the Banks of the Jordan British Nineteenth Century Painters*, by Kathy McLauchlan, 1986.

Brighton Museum and Manchester City Art Gallery, *The Inspiration of Egypt Its Influence on British Artists Travellers and Designers, 1700-1900*, edited by Patrick Conner, 1983.

Dublin, National Gallery of Ireland, and Liverpool, Walker Art Gallery, *The East Imagined, Experienced, Remembered Orientalist Nineteenth Century Painting*, by James Thompson, 1988.

Edinburgh, Talbot Rice Art Centre, and Norwich, Sainsbury Centre for the Visual Arts, *A Middle Eastern Journey Artists on their travels from the collection of Rodney Searight*, by Rodney Searight and Jennifer Scarce, 1980.

London, Barbican Art Gallery, *David Roberts*, compiled by Helen Guiterman and Briony Llewellyn, 1986.

London, Leighton House, *The Middle East Watercolours and drawings by British and foreign artists and travellers. 1750-1900. From the collection of Rodney Searight, Esq.*, by Rodney Searight, 1971.

London, Leighton House, *The Islamic Perspective An Aspect of British Architecture and Design in the 19th century*, by Michael Darby, 1983.

London, Leighton House, *Romantic Lebanon The European View 1700-1900*, edited by Briony Llewellyn, 1986.

London, Royal Academy of Arts, *The Orientalists: Delacroix to Matisse European Painters in North Africa and the Near East*, edited by MaryAnne Stevens, 1984.

London, Royal Academy of Arts, *Edward Lear 1812-1888*, by Vivien Noakes, 1985.

London, Victoria and Albert Museum, *The People & Places of Constantinople Watercolours by Amadeo Count Preziosi 1816-1882*, by Briony Llewellyn and Charles Newton, 1985.

New York, The Metropolitan Museum of Art, *The Image of the Turk in Europe*, by Alexandrine N.St.Clair, 1973.

Detailed bibliographies are to be found in the COMfiche catalogue of the Searight Collection.

Index of Artists

Joseph Marie Vien (1716-1809)

Trompettes, Pages, Esclaves, et Vases, que l'on portoit pour present, a Mahomet

Etching
20.5 x 13.4 cm.
Lettered with title and *Jos. Vien inv. Sc.*

This is the frontispiece to Vien's set of etchings, *Caravanne du Sultan a la Mecque,* which commemorated the masquerade staged by the students at the Académie Française for the annual carnival in Rome in 1748. The theme of the Sultan's entourage during his pilgrimage to Mecca provided the opportunity for a dazzling display of glittering costumes. The cavalcade was a huge success and received accolades from, amongst others, the French Ambassador, who wrote: 'More than forty different costumes were exhibited, representing every Eastern country as well as the principal personages at the Court of the Grand Seigneur. About twenty of them were on horseback, the rest in a carriage which they

had transformed into a magnificent wagon in shape and dimensions. Their clothes, though only linen, were so well painted that even from close up they could hardly have resembled more exactly the real materials and brocades. You really cannot imagine the applause that greeted this cavalcade (which is very much to the taste of this part of the world), as it passed along the Corso, alike from the people and from the nobility.' The masquerade was a manifestation of the 'turkomania' that gripped Europe in the mid-eighteenth century, and although the costumes were as fanciful as others in the Turkish style at that time, their abundance and variety were unusual.